A handbook of

ARTS & CRAFTS

For elementary and junior high school teachers

Third edition

Willard F. Wankelman
Philip Wigg
Marietta Wigg

Bowling Green University, Ohio

Wm. C. Brown Company, Publishers / Dubuque, Iowa

ART SERIES

Consulting Editor

Willard F. Wankelman
Bowling Green University

To
the memory
of
Marietta Wigg
coauthor,
colleague, and
wife

CONTENTS

PREFACE

The authors believe this, the third edition of *A Handbook of Arts and Crafts,* to be a considerable improvement over previous editions, and hope that this view is shared by their readers. Extensive changes have been made on the basis of the authors' own experiences in using the book as a classroom aid. In addition, other users who have made suggestions will often find many recommendations incorporated in the revision.

The authors do not believe in change for the sake of change. The basic content of the book, which has pleased many readers, has been left largely undisturbed. Most of the attention has been centered on making it more attractive and more usable. This has resulted in the addition of considerable color, some new illustrations, and extensive screening of the projects. Those projects which proved to be little-used have been replaced with other more effective projects.

The basic purpose of the book is unchanged; it is to offer direction and practical help to all who have any influence on the shaping of elementary and junior high school art programs. The role of art in the development of the total child has been increasingly understood in recent years, and this appreciation has resulted in the development of classroom problems of a creative nature. Many of these problems have been given publicity in art journals, and have become more or less standard teaching procedures; others have been developed spontaneously in the classroom as the result of particular needs. All of these problems are included in this book when they are considered to have value. The book, therefore, is *not* new "from cover to cover," but only in the sense that it contains carefully sifted problems representing the most recent professional attitudes toward the presentation of art at this level.

These attitudes, incidentally, are the core of the book to the extent that they can be communicated to the reader. The knowledge that they are vital but still unfamiliar to many involved in art instruction has prompted the inclusion of certain sections in the book. It is the belief of the writers that once a teacher has evolved a sound philosophy of art he will be able to turn any kind of assignment toward creative ends. Such a philosophy must include the recognition that in art, suggestion, not dictation, is the rule, and that creativity lies as much in the approach as in the results. Hence every teacher should use these problems according to the abilities of the individuals in his class. Variation on the problems is not only condoned, but encouraged, as possible applications are many. The goal of all educational processes is creative thinking, and art can be an invaluable aid to the teacher in working toward this desirable condition.

ART AND TEACHING

Basic Concepts of Art Instruction

One of the grave responsibilities of the day is borne by education, in providing youth with opportunities and guidance in the fulfillment of its creative powers. Technological advances of recent years have given us much in material comfort and also produced a situation in which the vast majority of our citizens passively accept the creative activities of a few. The basic creative impulse has been retarded in the individual, frustrating his opportunities for self-expression. Paradoxically, creativity has languished while its possibilities have increased. The shorter work-week produced by automation has left plenty of leisure time but offered little incentive for its effective use. Generally speaking, we are turning into a nation of watchers rather than doers—we ask to be entertained, not challenged into action. This is a situation which needs drastic over-hauling for the benefit of the individual and, in a larger sense, his world. Society is in great need of original thinking from its members.

If original thought is needed, there can be no place for the kind of teaching which cherishes the comforts of conformity and proceeds on the basis of formula, or predigested information. The only educational system of any value is one which can encourage open-minded curiosity and exploration. Students cannot really think until they are able to experiment with ideas and, by a process involving all their facilities, accept or reject them. Student thinking is often fallible—but mistakes made in the process of earnest searching are much more valuable than the "correct" answers to be found in formulas, formulas which guarantee a pre-determined form of success by placing a limit on the imagination.

Genuinely creative thinking, in any field, is done on an abstract level; it is a product of flights of fancy (of often seemingly ridiculous extremes), unlimited by practical considerations. In science, a realm of utilitarianism, there is a distinct difference between the "pure" and the "applied." Truly creative and significant ideas appear in "pure" science, whereas originality in "applied" science is usually limited to their practicalization. The most meaningful art forms have been born in an atmosphere of freedom of individual pursuit without the restrictions of usefulness or rules. The proper teaching of art then, must forget practicality if it hopes to develop any sensitivity to the true nature of art—it must try to evoke an appreciation for things in their own right.

The artist, amateur or professional, finds in art a medium in which he can create a world on his own terms. In his god-like role he can find therapy, solace, pleasure, and catharsis. The basic urge in art probably involves a communication of some kind. Regardless of the personality involved, however, the ultimate satisfaction is that it has forged its way through problems both physical and mental and brought about a conclusion which materializes as something uniquely its own.

Because of the expressive function of art, the basic philosophy of this book is in direct conflict with all practices which tend to standardize and stress application. Classroom use of hectographs, mimeographs, and coloring books discourage inventive and expressive ideas in the development of creative students. Oddly enough, the sins of copying are readily recognized aud forbidden in most areas of school study, but are often allowed, and even encouraged, in art. Presumably this situation exists because of two reasons: (1) although it is in fortunate decline, the feeling still persists that art is essentially an imitative or recreative process, and (2) the establishment of a creative classroom atmosphere involves a separate approach with each member of the class—a far more demanding task than the supplying of copy-work material.

The emphasis here placed on creative freedom thus far might be interpreted as an insistence on complete abandonment or, at best, pure abstraction in art. Regardless of its final form, all art is always somehow rooted in nature and is based on a wide variety of individual experiences. Both nature and personal experience are of tremendous complexity and subject to an infinite number of legitimate interpretations. The great latitude of approach deriving from the subjective character of the field can be, without proper supervision, an invitation to chaos, although discipline is of as great importance in art as in any field. Herein lies one important role of the teacher, that of understanding, assessing, and weighing spontaneity against discipline according to the needs and responsibilities of the individual student.

Where art is used as a tool for the investigation of subject areas such as history, etc., its unique properties are often sacrificed. When this happens, art becomes a mere reporting device. The value of art in a unit of study is always in direct proportion to the emphasis placed on original thinking; when art is made a slave to another study its essence is destroyed, and it is no longer art. Art should be used to throw fresh light

In decorating each fish the urge to create has carried this student beyond the limitations of this stereotyped classroom assignment.

on the academic by revealing hidden values through personal interpretation. In other words, art should operate on the basis of its own principles, not those of the subject being studied. If classroom experiences can be properly tied to creative art programs, both areas of study will be enriched. Art experience can be involved with every field of school work. History, science, geography, literature—all contain material around which art instruction could be organized.

Enthusiasm, in order to be perpetuated, must be shared. Most children have a natural excitement for art. Their first drawings seem to occur instinctively, and are very enjoyable and meaningful to them. Young people show a natural gift for expression which is unhampered by considerations of style or accuracy in the adult sense. When selected subjects are carefully fed into their absorbent minds and allowed to ferment, they reappear in marvelously fresh interpretations. The ideal teacher of art should have the mental flexibility which permits him to see and appreciate things under new and unique conditions. He should

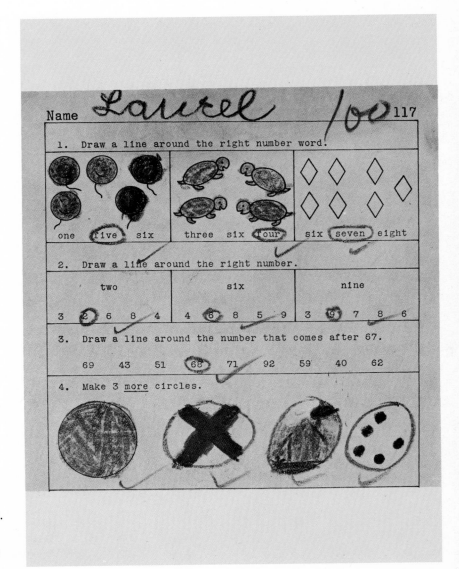

This illustration is evidence of a child's creative urge trying to find expression. Not being satisfied with the simple shapes required as answers, he has used them in creating houses, flowers and experimental designs.

also have an evident capacity for excitement which can match that of the student. A good art situation is a very remarkable thing—a mutually educative process for student and teacher.

We have spoken of the need for the preservation of the dignity of art as a basic discipline. If one reviews the history of art, beginning with the untutored but intensely felt drawings of primitive man, one cannot escape the conclusion that art is an elemental and necessary activity of the human animal. The things put down by prehistoric men—beasts, weapons, warriors, gods—are formed in a direct manner with natural response to color, rhythm, texture; the means of art are used in an uncomplicated way showing the close identification of the man with his subject and medium. The same immediacy is apparent when a child begins to draw: the tools—pencil, chalk, crayon—produce great joy as they are introduced, and the drawings created reflect this spirit. A torrent of work pours out representing all manner of things, but expressing one mood, that of an intoxication of interest in the marvels of the world. Subjects may change, the form of expression may change, but interest rarely flags until someone in authority begins to question the legitimacy of the images created, by comparing them to adult products. When this happens, the rapport between child and art breaks, adventure ceases, and the work becomes a labored parroting of tired examples.

Admittedly, the child's ultimate progress is toward adulthood, but must this natural process be unnaturally accelerated by frustration and inhibition? Does it seem reasonable that accuracy must be substituted for the appreciation of a beautiful color, a bold line, or a vibrant pattern? The need for accuracy will make itself felt in any event when the normal child reaches a certain emotional (not chronological) level. When the quest for realism occurs and when the child asks for help, it should be given, not as a manifesto, but as a gift which, if accepted, can exist without threatening the survival of his remaining creative resources.

The principles of art are those qualities which, in a very flexible degree and order, seem to be instrumental in making a work seem urgent and readable. When we were children, most of us responded quite naturally to rhythm, variety, repetition, balance, emphasis—pointing them out seemed a superfluous act. Unfortunately, the aging process, the complexities of society, including social and economic drives, soon supply us with a veneer of sophistication which blunts our responsiveness. We are afraid of failure and consequently shirk the attempt. There are so many opinions on subjects (and particularly art) that we adopt the safest one: we want clear-cut, decisive answers and tangible worthwhile goods—houses, washing machines, televisions—food for the stomach in preference to the psyche. It is no wonder that this materialistic infection can contaminate art to the extent that the principles which should serve to illuminate expression soon become rules which camouflage and disguise.

When, to what extent, and how are art principles to be applied in supervision so as to avoid the misunderstanding which could easily transmute them into rules? In the first place, children must accept criticism on their terms, that is, when they are prepared to weigh, judge, and apply it. Determination of this readiness must be made on an individual basis by a teacher who understands the personalities involved. As art is a type of personal expression, any suggestions should be advanced as possibilities to be evaluated in terms of their effect on this expression in the total work. Too many suggestions could easily dilute the individuality of the expression. It may be agreed that a better feeling may be produced through a change of color, that a different placement may heighten the action, that there is too much or too little concentration in certain areas—all of these involving degrees of contrast or sameness according to the general effect intended.

Respect for the individual and his ideas is a noble democratic sentiment and a cardinal code of conduct for the teacher who expects a genuine and sustained interest from art students. Maintenance of a socratic atmosphere of group debate and free evaluation insures a continuous outlet and discipline for creative impulses. A further requisite is recognition: conscientious effort in art nearly always produces some real merits in a work, regardless of its overall quality. Recognition of these merits should always be given priority in any comments; the younger the child the more emphatic the recognition given should be. As the child develops emotional maturity, criticism may become more pointed and specific, but should never be undiluted, nor should it ever include personal prejudice, sarcasm, or ridicule. A consuming interest in art can be completely aborted by a few intemperate words. There are undoubtedly vast resources of potential creativity which have been lost to us because of a well-meaning instructional faux pas.

The average teacher, even without benefit of specialized art training, is capable of stimulating and perpetuating creativity in children by applying simple principles of psychology. Deficiencies in training become monumentally important only if the teacher is unwilling to acknowledge them openly, and admit that he can learn something from his students. Professional knowledge of the field should be acquired, but this qualification is of far less importance than the attitude of the person involved. The attitude of the art teacher is always evident in the illustrations with which he surrounds his students. A sylvan glade by Corot, a seventeenth century Dutch still life, a Blue Boy by Gainsborough may all be good paintings, but have probably been seen so often that they are taken for granted. It is far better to have something which will attract attention and become a subject of controversy. Nothing is more healthy than argument if it is confined to logical premises; only by arguing a point can we come close to a determination of its validity. Art has never been intended to be taken for granted. A good art work has always been a product of the controversy raging in the artist's mind, and it has usually aroused some degree of controversy when submitted to the public. By displaying works which are little-known or stylistically strange, the teacher can augment the learning process, and keep the interest and creative freedom of the art class at a high level.

The history of art is normally associated with upper–level students, but there is no reason younger children should be excluded from the subject. Indeed, when one considers that art can be related to virtually every other subject, one can see that its history can be a germinal field for the study of man's past. The amazing developments in the color slides and prints today make quality reproductions from every period and source accessible to all. Opaque, overhead movie and slide projectors are now common items in the school inventory, featuring great fidelity and

Children are invariably fascinated by exotically unfamiliar forms of expression. . . .

ease of operation. Excellent films on art for various age groups are available through many sources.

All of these resources can be used along with, or in place of, trips to museums. Children are invariably fascinated by exotically unfamiliar forms of expression, and viewings of any kind should always be accompanied by an opportunity for discussion in which there is a prompting of speculation on why the artist works as he does. The period and country in which the artist worked will help to account for this, and will easily lead into some consideration of the many historical forces which shaped the style.

Study would necessarily have to be kept within the limits of student comprehension, but should be approached in an open-minded questioning manner to which the teacher can contribute some factual material. In such a way, the ageless reciprocity between history and art can be made an enlightening experience for student and teacher. It is also exciting, if somewhat unnerving, to discover the insight and empathy which youngsters display in their reaction to art, qualities which frequently outstrip those of their elders who, being somewhat jaded, are far less responsive and perceptive.

There is no place for the ritual of rote in art history for the young. Precise fact should defer to generalized example and the provocative and unfamiliar should be given priority over the taken-for-granted. Any information acquired should arise from initial reaction to the works themselves. This reaction should prompt questioning for which the instructor should be prepared; he should, if possible, draw answers out of the pupils themselves through group discussion.

Art history can excite the young into new torrents of creativity, demonstrate that the artist is mirror and barometer of his society, and reaffirm the old axiom that "man without man's past is meaningless."

The Art World of the Child

Any child is a personality separate and distinct from all others of his kind. He is an incalculably complex product of a combination of formative influences which can occur only once.

Despite his many individual qualities the child passes though definite cycles of development which are common to other children. Although these cycles are an inevitable part of growth, it is impossible to predict the time of their appearance or their duration. Stages are often catalogued according to chronological age, but this is only a measurement of convenience; actually, development is geared to emotional maturity, which varies from child to child.

It is very important for the teacher to understand and recognize cycles of child development as illustrated by the art work created. Each cycle is characterized by certain abilities and attitudes, to which the art activities of the individual should be geared.

Manipulative Stage

When art materials are first discovered by the child he will explore endlessly, usually producing results which are unintelligible by the average adult standards (Figs. 1, 2). For the child the joy of discovery is the thing; he is interested in seeing just what effects the media will produce. At times he gives every evidence of regarding it as a very serious business, and at other times he will shriek with joy. He will frequently accompany his explorations with a story of some kind, but the subjects of his story will rarely be recognizable in his work. The child is always completely absorbed, and is having fun, but he is also perfecting his coordination, discovering the world through new correlations, and learning the possibilities of new materials.

Figure 1. "House with Decoration" by four-year-old child.

Figure 2. A collage titled "Just for Fun" by a five-year-old child.

When art materials are first discovered by the child he will explore endlessly, usually producing results which are unintelligible by the average adult standards.

Symbolic Stage

As the child continues to experiment he will eventually discover his ability to produce likenesses (Fig. 3). The images are not at all sophisticated, and may seem crude and inaccurately observed. Actually, visual correlations are not important to him, and his observation is very keen in terms of his experience with things. The logic in the work is in terms of what he knows about his subjects. For example, the scale of an object or person is in proportion to the importance which he attaches to it.

The child's interest in space is strictly limited to the flatness of the working surface. Things are freely rearranged according to an instinctive feeling for design, and because they make a more tangible representation of his experiences with them. In Fig. 4 the sun is moved to the ground level, the man's hat is floating near the top of the page, and his mouth is made extremely large (because he was calling his son). In the symbolic stage the child often uses recognizable images, but only as a means to an end—the end in this case being self-expression.

If the teacher insists on realism for its own sake the expressive **role of** art is lost. The child has no comprehension of, or interest in, realism *per se.* Fig. 5 is a standard hectograph picture in which the creativity of the child is limited to the application of color to prefabricated adult images. Fig. 6, on the other hand, has been freely produced by the child on the basis of his own observations and decisions. It represents a child in a playground, with slides and swings floating in the sky.

Representations of trains are made in the next reproductions (Figs. 7, 8). The first drawing has been made in tempera paint and the second in pencil. The pencil drawing combines the most representative views of train and tracks, the train being in profile, and the tracks as if seen from

Figure 3. "Roy Had a Cold and Had to Stay in the House."

Figure 4. "A Man Calling His Son."

The scale of an object or person is in proportion to the importance which the child attaches to it.

Figure 5. A hectographed adult image.

Figure 6. "A Child in a Playground with Slides and Swings."

above. Both are aspects of the subjects which are most frequently observed. No effort has been made to integrate them into one common viewpoint. The tempera painting shows rain falling. The sky is represented by a symbol, a stripe across the top of the page. Such symbols are common in child art and, as far as the children are concerned, are perfectly adequate. Because of the use of such symbolic devices the art work of the young is usually very simple, having been abstracted down to a few essentials. They are excellent examples of brevity. They also exemplify expressive use of color; colors are used fearlessly, and fully in context with the mood of the artist.

Figure 7. Representation of a train made with tempera paint.

Figure 8. Pencil representation of a train in profile with tracks as if seen from above.

Realistic Stage

With increasing maturity, and usually beginning at ages seven to ten, the child becomes more factually oriented (Fig. 9). He becomes more conscious of adult protoypes and with his increasing coordination begins to wonder about his ability to produce things more realistically. He is, however, still a child, and unable to cope with adult standards. If the teacher preaches the virtues of realism at this emotional level the results could be disastrous. Far better to point out that professional artists do not feel impelled to work realistically, and that expression is the main purpose of art.

As the child grows into adolescence, misconceptions about the proper place of realism and technique become magnified. It is a period of insecurity in which he gradually becomes aware of the vast complexities of the world, and his own limitations in relation to them. He becomes thirsty for factual knowledge. Actual information about things is important to him before he will attempt to draw them. This is a very critical period for student and teacher alike. The child's feelings of inferiority call for constant encouragement and sympathetic understanding. It is important that he be guided in such a subtle way that he feels he is finding his own answers—this will buoy up his self-confidence. More than any other, this level of development calls for teachers with a good background in art, who understand the field so well that they can constantly provide a stimulus through the introduction of new materials, techniques, and illustrations. It is important for the child to see, with his own eyes, that artists have always been most successful when they have remained true to themselves, when they have evolved a truly personal style based on a thorough knowledge of the styles of other artists.

Figure 9. With increasing maturity the child becomes more factually oriented. In this illustration the child is beginning to show some awareness of the distances which separate objects from each other, but is still unable to relate things in terms of their usual proportions.

Positive and Negative Suggestions on Creative Art Teaching

The following remarks are intended primarily for the classroom teacher who has little specialized instruction in the methods of teaching art. If the suggestions often seem contradictory, it is because no exact recommendation can always be provided for a situation, nor can every situation be anticipated. Effectiveness in art teaching, as in any other form of teaching, eventually focuses on the individual teacher's judgment and taste. These comments should therefore be regarded as suggestions, not admonitions. They are included to suggest some of the effective methods and attitudes that are peculiar to the field of art. Perhaps the most important of these is the reminder that an art class is a workshop of ideas and materials, not a standard lecture recitation situation. In such an environment over-guidance is probably worse than under-guidance, and rules, formulas and the "tried and true" are of little value.

Positive

Allow the child free rein in expression; for him art may be the means to several goals, some of which are:

1. A feeling of self-confidence in having control of his materials.
2. A means through which he may express himself more fully than in other media.
3. A way of better understanding the world and his place in it.
4. The satisfaction (rarely obtained these days) which comes with the expression of the basic creative impulse latent in all of us.

Use art as an integral part of the day's activities. Demonstrate an active and sincere interest in the things being done.

Understand that children create emotionally and intellectually. Their works are illustrative of their deepest feelings and as such are deserving of sympathetic understanding, not criticism.

Children are only interested in demonstrating the reality of the mind and emotions, not the reality of outward appearances.

Children need a certain degree of privacy; give them a feeling of independence.

Children are sensitive creatures; show equal appreciation and concern for all the members of the class.

Give the student an opportunity to have contact with art products of all ages. Show catholicity of taste. Let him develop a long-lasting appreciation of art based on his own considered judgments, but see to it honest consideration is given in every case.

Negative

Avoid the imposition of a subject unless the child is completely without ideas; if so, merely suggest, don't prescribe.

Don't create the impression that art is merely "busy work" or a time-filler. Don't set the wheels in motion and turn your attention to other matters.

Don't be surprised by the ideas which pour out of the efforts of the very young, and don't criticize them, even if they prove embarrassing. The children are merely reflecting the events around them and their reactions to them.

Don't worry about the objects drawn or the method of depiction until the students reach an age level at which it is natural for them to seek help.

Don't hover over the child exhibiting anxiety over the outcome of his work.

When using student works as examples, try to show them in such a way as to avoid extremes of praise or fault-finding.

Don't limit the child's art consumption to the styles for which you may happen to have a personal preference.

Negative

Don't always expect the student to show enthusiasm for subjects which are totally unrelated to his own life situations.

Don't isolate pupils from each other, or discourage a certain amount of conversation if it is of a constructive nature.

Don't let freedom of expression lead to abandonment of good work habits.

Discourage copying and reliance on rules and formulas whenever possible.

Avoid the use of trite, unimaginative, and outdated pictures and materials in the classroom.

Art should not be pigeon-holed and isolated from other areas. Its concern is man and his total existence.

Don't relinquish your responsibility in the teaching of art to another person, unless that person's credentials as an art teacher are clearly superior to your own.

Don't expect precise, accurate, academic drawings of stereotyped objects. Such drawings have limited value only for more mature individuals.

Don't expect complete self-reliance from immature children, or feel that their ideas will be inexhaustible.

Positive

Relate your art instruction to those things which are part of the child's own experiences.

Encourage children to show and explain their work to others in the class, creating an atmosphere of mutual interest.

Maintain certain standards in regard to the care of materials and the cleanliness of work area and person.

Attach fundamental importance to creativity and individual thinking.

Teach the child to develop taste by making use of good design principles in bulletin boards and other displays. Emphasize the art concepts of the twentieth century wherever possible.

Point out correlations and relationships in art works and between art and other fields. Help make art a vital part of an awakening process.

If you have had any experience in art which gives you any confidence in your teaching, do your own art teaching. Elementary art is primarily a matter of guidance and encouragement, and you can provide this for your own people better than anyone else if you take the trouble to acquaint yourself with the fundamental art concepts.

Encourage pictorial ideas based on personal activities.

Lend sympathetic assistance to those who don't know where to go with their work. Children expect and deserve help occasionally—this in art is usualy a matter of motivation by "talking it over."

Positive

Stress the use of class art problems which involve a minimum of instruction. These should stimulate the student's appreciation for visual effects and afford an opportunity for exploration.

Treat each person as a unique personality. Encourage him to reveal himself in his art, and try to understand him and his problems better from this revelation through his work.

Let the child do his own work; give him the immense satisfaction that comes from having been solely responsible for the conception and execution of a piece of work.

Expect and encourage greater informality during the class art period. Real art is a matter of expression and cannot flourish under duress. It depends on a contagion of the spirit and a free exchange of ideas.

Permit the child to grapple with problems occasionally. Let him see that the degree of success is often in direct proportion to the amount of perspiration expended, and that the greatest art works frequently seem simple only because the artist has had the judgment and patience to reduce things to elementals.

Use constructive criticism. Instead of saying "that's bad" try to find a solid solution, or imply that something else might work better.

Be honest with yourself and the children. Admit to them that the happy results of the art projects occur as an accident, or as a result of the special disciplines of the projects.

Allow the child to progress according to his ability.

Ration the time according to the complexities of the activity.

Use all available visual aids which are of good quality. These will serve as an effective stimulus.

Negative

By all means avoid the use of ready-made art techniques, such as coloring books, number paintaing, etc. Such devices slam the door on sensitivity and originality, and make art a lifeless mechanical routine.

One cannot expect identical or even very similar results from the diverse personalities normally encountered in the classrooms. Don't demand conformity.

Don't work on a student's product, unless he asks to see something demonstrated, and do not, if you draw on his work, make it a formula for him to copy.

Don't discourage conversation and a certain degree of class motion.

Don't create the impression that art is child's play in its entirety, or that creation is always unalloyed fun.

Don't lavish praise on the child to the extent that he begins to expect acknowledgment of his genius.

Don't always confuse results with intentions. Accept results if they turn out well, but point out that there comes a time when end-products are not enough.

Don't try to force gifted or retarded children into the same mold with the normal children. Try to set up special activities for those whose talents are extraordinarily great or small.

The child should not be "turned off" when he is beginning to respond, nor should he have time left over for distractions.

Don't always expect ideas to flow in a torrent. There are fertile and infertile periods in any child's creativity.

BULLETIN BOARDS

Effective Use of the Bulletin Board

Bulletin boards can make learning a pleasure for the child by surrounding him with stimulating and decorative displays. All areas of school study can profit by a creative presentation of subject material.

Bulletin boards should be changed frequently to continue to retain the child's interest, the frequency of change depending upon a great many intangibles; the interest period of pictorial matter is generally shorter than that of a more technical nature. The teacher will have to sense the saturation point and make arrangements for new displays. He should make sure that out-of-date material is removed immediately, and that items of timely interest are posted promptly.

In addition to their usefulness in the classroom bulletin boards can announce events and record activities of general interest. In so doing they also help to enrich halls and corridors and intensify school spirit.

The effectiveness of a bulletin board, regardless of its content, depends upon its arrangement. Arranging a display on a bulletin board is a problem in designing which includes consideration of size, shape, color, texture, value, variety, balance and repetition.

The following brief suggestions will be of some help in developing a successful display.

1. Harmonize the shapes to be placed on the bulletin board with the structural lines of the board as shown in the illustration directly below.

2. The busyness of the arrangement confuses the basic purpose of a bulletin board—communication.

3. The background area around the shapes placed on the bulletin board should be as interesting as the shapes themselves.

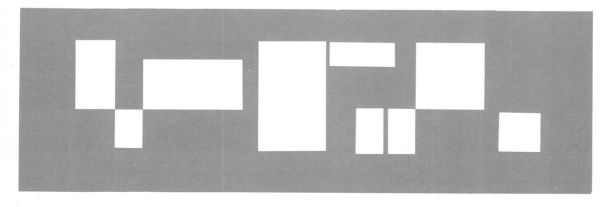

4. Always allow a larger margin at the bottom than at the top or sides. This principle also applies to the matting of pictures (see pages 112–14).

5. One color or texture distributed throughout the display can serve to unify the bulletin board. This is easily accomplished by mounting the subjects on a particular color or textured surface.

6. Think of the space to be decorated as if it were a scale, and balance formally or informally as shown.

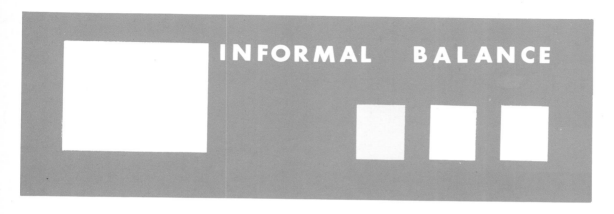

7. If lettering is to be incorporated in the display it should be legible and concise—one or two words, a short phrase, or a short question. A title is of little value if it cannot be read quickly. Lettering should be considered an integral part of every display, but avoid lettering that must be read on a diagonal or from top to bottom.

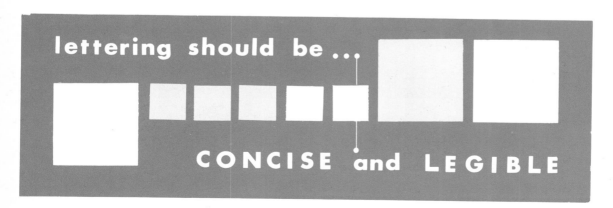

8. If lettering must be used other than horizontal, make it read from the bottom up. (See following illustration to avoid any misunderstanding.) The style of the lettering should also be kept simple.

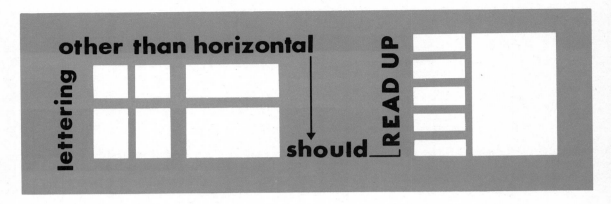

9. Colored string, yarn, or ribbon can be tacked or pinned into place to control the desired eye movement by leading the observer through the arrangement.

10. Group the material to be displayed on the bulletin board by **topic** or related subjects.

11. Bulletin boards lend themselves to the display of every **school or** extracurricular activity. However, if class work or art work is to be displayed, be sure each child is represented.

12. Displays do not have to be limited to flat items; shadow boxes, paper sculpture, or any other three-dimensional objects may be attached to the board, and may be included as part of a display merely to create variety and attract attention.

13. It is better to have no board at all than to have one which is overburdened. Allow comfortable intervals between notices or displays.

CERAMICS

Clay Modeling

Supplies

1. Local or commercial water base clay

Procedure

Method A

1. Beginning with a basic shape of the object to be modeled, squeeze or push the clay to form the features (legs, arms, head, etc.). Think of the object as a whole, rather than as separate parts.
2. Allow the piece to dry slowly at room temperature.
3. Check pages 27 and 28 for firing details.

Method B

1. Beginning with a basic shape of the object to be modeled, use a modeling tool to carve away all unnecessary parts until the piece is formed.

NOTE: Combining parts or sections is another method of modeling, but not recommended for children. Assembling parts is very important, and unless the two pieces of clay are of the same consistency, and combined together properly, they will shrink irregularly in drying.

Clay Tiles

Procedure

1. Knead (wedge) the clay to a workable consistency.
2. Spread the damp cloth on a smooth table top.
3. Place the two sticks on the damp cloth parallel to each other. The space between the sticks will be the width of the finished tile.

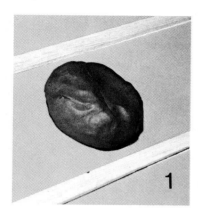

4. Roll a ball of clay and place it between the sticks (Ill. 1).

5. Flatten the clay by running the rolling pin along the parallel sticks. The clay will be flattened to the thickness of the sticks (Ill. 2).

6. Cut the slab of clay into tiles, and allow it to become almost dry, or leather-hard (Ill. 3).

7. Plan a design on thin paper, the size of the clay tile.

Supplies

1. Local or commercial water base clay
2. Rolling pin
3. Two sticks, one-half inch thick
4. Damp cloth
5. Knife or scissors
6. Thin paper
7. Sharp pencil

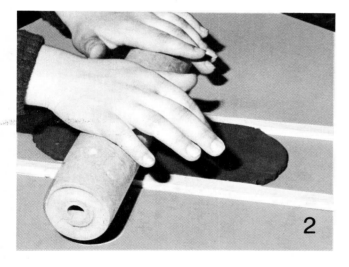

8. When the clay is almost dry, place the paper design over the tile, and transfer the design by retracing the lines with a sharp pencil or instrument.

9. The following three methods of decoration are possible:

   a) Incised—scratch the design into the leather-hard clay with a sharp tool.
   b) Relief—carve away the background areas and allow the design to stand out.
   c) Inlaid—carve out areas of the design and replace with clay of a different color, making sure both clays are of the same consistency.

10. See pages 27 and 28 for firing details.

Coil Pot

Supplies

1. Local or commercial water base clay
2. Modeling tool
3. Small container for mixing slip

Procedure

Method A

(Coils built on a pinch pot base as done by the American Indians)

1. Knead (wedge) the clay to a workable consistency.
2. Roll a ball of pliable clay between the palms of the hands to form a sphere approximately the size of a small orange.
3. Hold the sphere in the fingers of both hands. The thumb should be free to press the clay to form the pot. Keep thumbs pointed up and form the pot upside down.
4. Press the thumbs gently into the center of the sphere and at the same time press with the fingers on the outside while rotating the ball of clay (Ill. 1).
5. Continue pressing with both the fingers and the thumbs while rotating the clay until the ball is hollowed and the walls are of uniform thickness (approximately one-half of an inch). Cracks may appear if the clay is too dry, or if pressed into shape too quickly or forcefully. Repair any such cracks immediately by gently rubbing the fingers over the clay until they disappear.
6. The pot, if built correctly, will not have any flat areas. To flatten the bottom of the pot, hold it gently between the fingers with both hands and tap it lightly on a table top.
7. Roll another piece of clay into round strips or coils of approximately one-half of an inch in diameter, making sure the strip makes a complete turn to insure its roundness (Ill. 2).
8. Scratch the top edge of the pinch pot base (Ill. 3) and apply a thin coat of slip (liquid clay) over the scratches (Ill. 4). The slip helps the coil adhere to the pinch pot base.
9. Place the coil on the slip-covered edge of the base (Ill. 5). Cut both ends at the same angle so that they fit snugly (Ill. 6). Gently press the coil to the base and fuse the joint both on the outside and inside (Ill. 7).
10. Scratch the top edge of the first coil, apply slip (Ill. 8) and add the second coil. Remember to fit the ends together tightly. Gently press the second coil to the first coil and fuse them together.

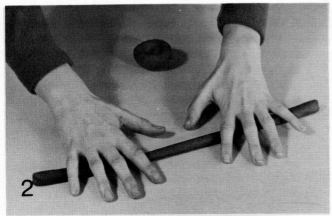

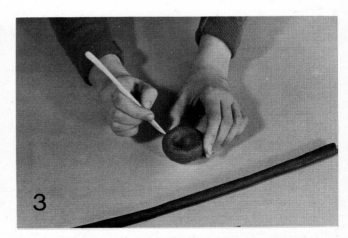

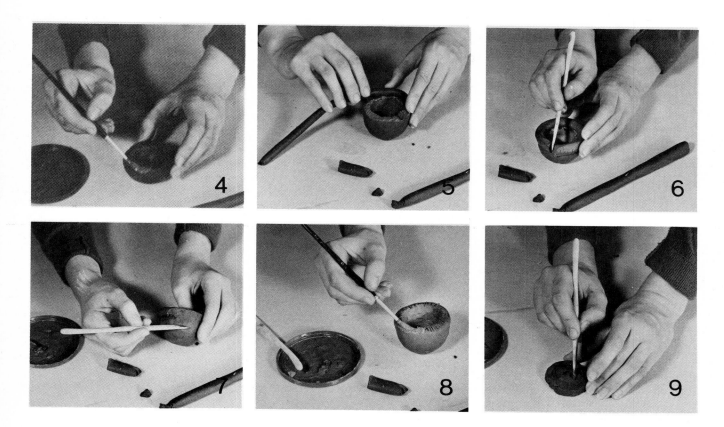

11. Repeat procedure ten until the coils create a completed form.
12. Allow the pot to dry slowly at room temperature.
13. Check pages 27 and 28 for firing details.

Method B

1. Knead (wedge) the clay to a workable consistency.
2. Roll the clay into round strips or coils of approximately one-half of an inch in diameter, making sure the strip makes a complete turn to insure its roundness (Ill. 2).
3. Wind the strip into a tight coil to the desired size for the base. Fuse the coil together with a small tool or the fingers, until all traces of the round strip disappear (Ill. 9). A ball of clay flattened on a damp cloth to approximately one-half of an inch thickness also makes a good base for a pot when cut to the desired diameter.
4. Scratch the outside top edge of the base and apply a thin coat of slip (liquid clay) over the scratches. The slip helps the base adhere to the first coil.
5. Place another coil on the slip-covered edge of the base. Cut both ends at the same angle so they fit snugly. Gently press the coil to the base and fuse the joint both on the outside and inside.
6. Scratch the top edge of the first coil, apply slip and add the second coil. Remember to fit the ends together tightly. Gently press the second coil to the first coil and fuse them together.
7. Repeat procedure six until the coils create a complete form.
8. Allow the pot to dry slowly at room temperature.
9. Check pages 27 and 28 for firing details.

Folded Clay Animals

Supplies

1. Local or commercial water base clay
2. Rolling pin
3. Cloth
4. Knife
5. Two flat sticks, one-half inch thick
6. Paper, pencil, and scissors

Procedure

1. Knead (wedge) the clay to a workable consistency.
2. Spread a damp cloth on a smooth table top. Place the two sticks parallel to each other on the damp cloth. The distance between the sticks will determine the size of the finished animal.
3. Roll a ball of clay between the palms of the hands to form a sphere and place it between the sticks.
4. Flatten the ball of clay by running the rolling pin along the parallel sticks. The thickness of the clay is determined by the thickness of the sticks.
5. Draw an animal on a piece of paper which is the size of the clay slab. If desired, the drawing can be scratched directly on the clay.
6. Cut the animal pattern out of the paper and place it on the slab of clay.
7. Hold the paper in place and cut the clay with a knife, following the outline of the pattern (Ill. 1).
8. Gently remove the clay animal from the slab and curve it into position (Ill. 2). The legs will be bent down to make it a self-supporting unit. Parts of the clay animal can be twisted into various attitudes.
9. Smooth out any rough edges and add textures or features with any modeling tool.
10. If the clay is too soft to support itself, prop it up with a wad of paper or clay.
11. Allow the animal to dry slowly at room temperature (Ill. 3).
12. See pages 27 and 28 for firing suggestions.

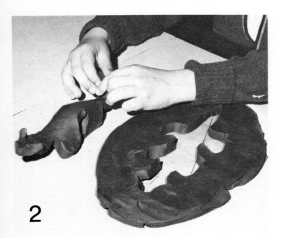

Kilns

Clay pieces that have just been completed are called *greenware* and should dry naturally before being fired in a kiln. Artificial heat is likely to cause the piece to crack. All decorations must be completed on the product before the piece is completely dry.

When the clay is completely dry (bone dry), it is ready to be placed in the kiln for firing. Firing will not only vitrify, or fuse, the clay, but will burn out any impurities.

There are numerous kilns of all sizes, shapes, and prices, which are fueled with gas, oil, coal or electricity. Small electric table model kilns that will operate on 110 to 115 volts and have a front door opening are suggested, and they, too, come in various sizes (Ill. 1.)

The inside firing chambers of table model kilns have a large range and usually a maximum of 2300°F, which is more than adequate. Several inside firing chamber sizes of electric table model kilns are:

$6\frac{1}{4}''$ wide, 7" deep, 4" high
6" wide, 6" deep, 6" high
8" wide, 10" deep, 4" high
10" wide, 12" deep, 5" high
10" wide, 9" deep, 10" high
10" wide, 10" deep, 9" high

Larger electric kilns will in all probability use 220 volt current.

Some kilns will have a switch control for low, medium, and high temperatures (Ill. 2). Some will come equipped with a pyrometer, an indicator for reading the kiln temperature (Ill. 3). These extras are ideal, but much cheaper and equally accurate are pyrometric cones (Ill. 4) which are used to indicate fusion.

Supplies

1. Kiln
2. Kiln shelves
3. Shelf supports
4. Kiln furniture (stilts, triangles)
5. Pyrometric cones
6. Kiln wash (Glaze drippings are easily removed from shelves coated with kiln wash.)
7. Kiln cement (for repairing cracks and chips in kiln wall)

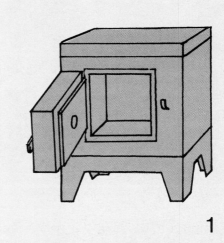

1

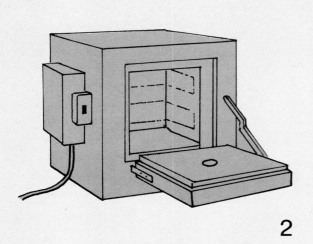

2

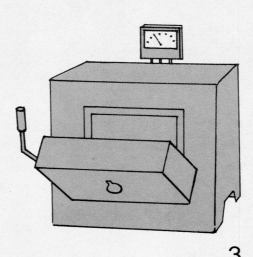

3

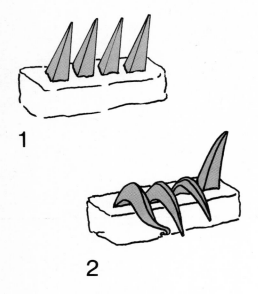

1

2

Three or four of these cones with different fusing points are placed at a slight angle to one of their faces (not on their edge) in a piece of pliable clay (Ill. 4). The clay is allowed to dry, then placed in the kiln so the cones can be seen through the spy-hole in the kiln door. A piece of fire brick may be necessary to lift the cones high enough to be seen.

The kiln will heat slowly and a periodic check of the cones through the spy-hole will let you know the approximate temperature of the heat as the cones begin to melt. When the last cone (Ill. 5) is beginning to melt, the kiln can be turned off, as the desired temperature has been attained.

Cone Temperature Chart

PYROMETRIC CONES

Cone Temperature Chart—Degrees Fahrenheit

Cone 018	1328	Cone 05	1904
Cone 016	1463	Cone 04	1940
Cone 015	1481	Cone 03	2039
Cone 014	1526	Cone 02	2057
Cone 013	1580	Cone 01	2093
Cone 012	1607	Cone 1	2120
Cone 011	1643	Cone 2	2129
Cone 010	1661	Cone 3	2138
Cone 09	1706	Cone 4	2174
Cone 08	1742	Cone 5	2201
Cone 07	1814	Cone 6	2246
Cone 06	1859		

Temperature equivalents figured at firing rate of 300° F per hour.

A piece fired only once is called *bisque,* or biscuit ware, and it can be glazed and fired again. A glaze will give the pieces a glasslike finish. Glazes can be purchased from a commercial company which will give instructions for use and the temperature cone at which the glaze matures. (Avoid any glazes not certified by the manufacturer as being free of lead and nontoxic.) The glaze is applied by spraying, brushing, or dipping. Dipping a piece in and out of a bowl of glaze may be the most practical method. Finger-marks are removed by daubing glaze on the spots with a brush.

Making Clay

Supplies

1. Local or commercial water base clay
2. Two containers for mixing clay (galvanized or plastic buckets, crocks, earthenware crocks, etc. A tightly fitting lid is desirable.)
3. Hammer or mallet
4. Cloth bag
5. Sieve, or piece of window screen
6. Plastic bags or aluminum foil for storing clay
7. A plaster slab is ideal for absorbing excess moisture from the clay

Any local clay can be easily transformed into pliable clay for classroom use by the following method. This same method is used in reconditioning any unfired clay.

Procedure

1. Break the moist clay into small pieces and allow them to dry thoroughly.
2. Place the pieces of dry clay into the cloth bag and pound them with the hammer or mallet until they are almost powder.
3. Fill the container half full of water and pour the broken or powdered clay into it until the clay rises above the surface of the water. Moist clay will not disintegrate when placed in water, so be sure it is bone dry and broken into pieces. The smaller the pieces, the more quickly the dissolving process will take place. This process is called *slaking.*

4. Allow the clay to soak for at least an hour. This period will vary according to the size of the pieces.
5. Stir the clay thoroughly with a stick or the hands until all the lumps are dissolved. This clay mixture is called *slip*.
6. Pour the slip into the second container through the sieve to remove any foreign matter and allow it to stand overnight. If there is any excess clear water, pour it off.
7. Remove any excess moisture by placing the clay on the plaster slab. Allow the water to be absorbed until the clay can be kneaded without sticking to the hands.
8. Store the clay in a container with a lid, or cover the container with a damp cloth. Small amounts of clay can be kept moist by using plastic bags or aluminum foil.

Suggestions on Handling Water Clay

1. Pliable clay should be kneaded (wedged) to remove all air bubbles before working.
2. Clay objects should dry slowly to prevent cracking. Thinner forms will dry more quickly than thicker forms. The thin form may be wrapped with a damp cloth to equalize the drying.
3. Cover the clay objects with a damp cloth or plastic bag to slow the drying process, or to keep the clay moist from day to day.
4. Moist clay will not adhere to dry clay due to shrinkage.
5. Clay appendages, or details which are to be added to pots or figures, must be of the same consistency as the piece to which they are to be attached. The two areas which are to be joined should be scratched with a tool, and covered with a slip (liquid clay) before being placed together. Then the joints should be fused into one piece with a smooth tool or the fingers.
6. If hanging plaques are to be made, carve or pierce any holes while the clay is leather-hard.
7. Dray clay objects (unfired clay is called greenware) must be fired to a temperature of at least 1500°F to be hardened. An electric kiln is the best method for firing. However, the primitve method of an open campfire can be utilized.
8. Glaze can be applied to bisque (a piece of clay which has been fired once is called bisque) by dipping, spraying, or with a brush. The piece is then refired. All glaze must be wiped from the bottom or the foot of the piece with a sponge or cloth before firing.
9. A simple low-fire glaze can be purchased commercially.
10. If no kiln is available, the greenware can be finished by waxing, painting with enamel, shellac or varnish, or with tempera paint. Clear plastic spray, varnish, or shellac can be applied over the tempera paint for permanency.
11. Slip (liquid clay) of different colors can be painted on damp-ware for decoration. The piece must then be dried and fired.
12. Overhandling of the clay will cause it to dry rapidly, which in turn causes cracks or crumbling.

Pinch Pot

Supplies

1. Local or commercial water base clay

Procedure

1. Knead (wedge) the clay to a workable consistency.
2. Roll a ball of pliable clay between the palms of the hands to form a sphere approximately the size of a small orange.
3. Hold the sphere in the fingers of both hands. The thumb should be free to press the clay to form the pot. Keep the thumbs pointed up and form the pot upside down. (See Ill. 1, p. 24.)
4. Press the thumbs gently into the center of the sphere and at the same time press with the fingers on the outside while rotating the ball of clay.
5. Continue pressing with both the fingers and thumbs while rotating the clay until the ball is hollowed and the walls are of uniform thickness (approximately one-half of an inch). Cracks may appear if the clay is too dry, or if it is pressed into shape too quickly or forcefully. Repair any such cracks immediately by gently rubbing the fingers over the clay until they disappear.
6. The finished pot, if built correctly, will not have any flat areas. To flatten the bottom of the pot, hold it gently between the fingers with both hands and tap it lightly on a table top.
7. Press the end of a key, hairpin, paper clip, etc., into the top edge of the pot, creating a single and interesting decoration.
8. Allow the pinch pot to dry slowly at room temperature.
9. See pages 27 and 28 for firing details.

Slab Pot

A slab pot is built with flat pieces of clay which are joined together to form a container.

Procedure

1. Knead (wedge) the clay to a workable consistency.
2. Spread the damp cloth on a smooth table top.
3. Place the two sticks on the damp cloth, parallel to each other. The space between the sticks will be the width of the finished tile.
4. Roll a ball of clay and place it between the sticks (Ill. 1).
5. Flatten the clay by running the rolling pin along the parallel sticks (Ill. 2). The clay will be flattened to the thickness of the sticks.
6. Place cardboard pattern over flattened clay. Using it as a guide, cut around pattern with a knife (Ill. 3).
7. Using the same cardboard pattern, cut three more slabs and allow to stiffen to a leather-hard condition.
8. To assemble a pot, score the edge of each slab with a knife (Ill. 4).
9. Put slip on scored edge (Ill. 5) and place two pieces together.
10. Prepare a small roll of clay and press into the joint of each corner Ill. 6). Continue this procedure until all four sides are together and smoothed inside and out.
11. Score the edges of a fifth piece, which will be the bottom.
12. Press the four sides on the bottom and complete (Ill. 7).

A cylindrical slab pot is made from one slab (Ill. 8) placed on a round base (Ill. 9).

Decorations can be done with a syringe filled with slip of a different color. Squeeze syringe and trail design.

Stamp any design in leather-hard clay.

Supplies

1. Local or commercial water base clay
2. Rolling pin
3. Two sticks, approximately ½ inch thick and 12 to 20 inches long
4. Damp cloth
5. Knife or scissors
6. Water container for mixing slip
7. Cardboard pattern

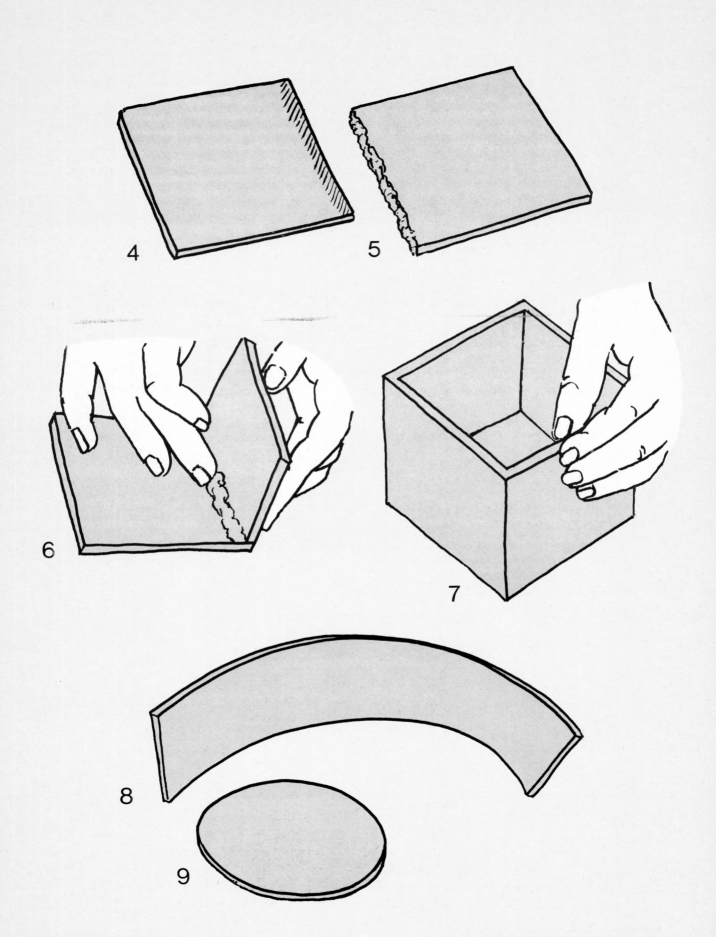

4

5

6

7

8

9

CHALK

Nature of the Medium

Chalk and Pastel

The original chalks for drawing, some still in use today, were pure earth, cut and shaped into implements. The addition of a binder created a fabricated chalk which we know as pastel. Sanguine Conté closely approximates the pure earth material. Chalks used by the early masters were generally limited to reds (sanguine), black, and white. These colors have been greatly increased in number.

Some artists apply chalks in separate strokes, letting the color blending take place in the viewer's eye. Others are not reluctant to blend the colors, and do so successfully, although there is a danger of the colors being muddied. Of course, there is no need to caution children against this; they should be encouraged to explore by rubbing with fingers, stumps, cotton swabs, anything available. Most children will select and use chalks fearlessly.

Chalk drawing is best done on a paper with "tooth," or a slightly coarse, abrasive surface. This texture helps the paper trap and hold the chalk particles. Many papers have this character, including the inexpensive manila.

Chalks are brittle, and easily broken. They are also impermanent, smearing very easily. Completed works should be sprayed with a protective fixative.

Chalks possessing strong color and binding ingredients should not be used on chalkboards—they are nearly indelible.

Chalk strokes can be strengthened, and their character altered, by wetting the chalk or paper. Various liquids have been used experimentally with interesting results, including dipping the chalk sticks in buttermilk, starch, and sugar water.

Chalk and Carbon Paper

Supplies

1. Paper
2. Carbon paper
3. Chalk
4. Clear spray

Procedure

1. Draw picture design on paper with colored chalk.
2. Place carbon paper face down on chalk drawing.
3. Run hand over carbon paper to transfer chalk drawing to carbon paper.
4. Remove carbon paper and spray with clear spray to keep from smearing.

Chalk and String Design

Supplies

1. String
2. Chalk
3. Soft wooden board
4. Thumbtacks
5. Paper
6. Plastic spray or fixative

Procedure

1. Press a tack into the board.
2. Tie string to the tack.
3. Rub the string with a piece of chalk.
4. Place the string over a sheet of paper, pull the string taut with one hand, and snap the string against the paper with the other hand.
5. Move the paper into different positions and repeat steps three and four after each movement of the paper.

NOTE: Assorted colors may be rubbed against the strings. Lines may be intentionally blurred by stroking. Shapes bounded by the lines may be colored in to create a more definite pattern. The chalk should be "fixed" to the paper with a protective coating of clear plastic spray or fixative.

Chalk and Tempera Paint

Procedure

1. Make a light pencil outline drawing on paper.
2. Mix tempera or latex paint to a consistency of cream.
3. Dip end of desired colored chalk into chosen color of paint.
4. Apply paint with chalk stick in brushlike strokes.
5. Continue until picture is completed.
6. Detail can be added with plain chalk.
7. Protect the picture with transparent spray.

Supplies

1. Chalk
2. Tempera, or latex paint
3. Paper
4. Clear spray

Chalk and Tempera Print

Procedure

1. Complete a design or drawing with colored chalk on a piece of good quality paper. Be sure to use the chalk heavily.
2. Coat another piece of paper of the same size with white tempera paint. Use a large brush and paint in both directions to smooth the paint over one entire side.
3. While the tempera is still wet, place the chalk drawing face down in the tempera paint.
4. Rub firmly over the paper with fingers and/or the hand.
5. Separate the two papers before they are dry.
6. Two prints will result—the chalk will have merged with the paint on both prints (Ill. 1, 2).
7. Experiments with different colors will produce numerous effects.

Supplies

1. Chalk
2. Tempera paint
3. Paper
4. Large brush

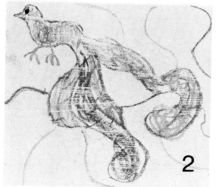

Chalk Textures

Supplies

1. Chalk
2. Thin drawing paper
3. Pencil
4. Textured surfaces

Procedure

1. Hold a thin paper against a surface which has a definite texture and rub the chalk over the paper. The texture will be transferred to the paper by the chalk.
2. Place the paper against another texture and transfer it to another portion of the paper.
3. Textures may be overlapped.

NOTE: A number of suggested textural surfaces are shown below. Chalk is easily smeared, and the completed drawing should have some protection. Commercially manufactured transparent sprays and fixatives are of some help, as is a home recipe to be found on page 246.

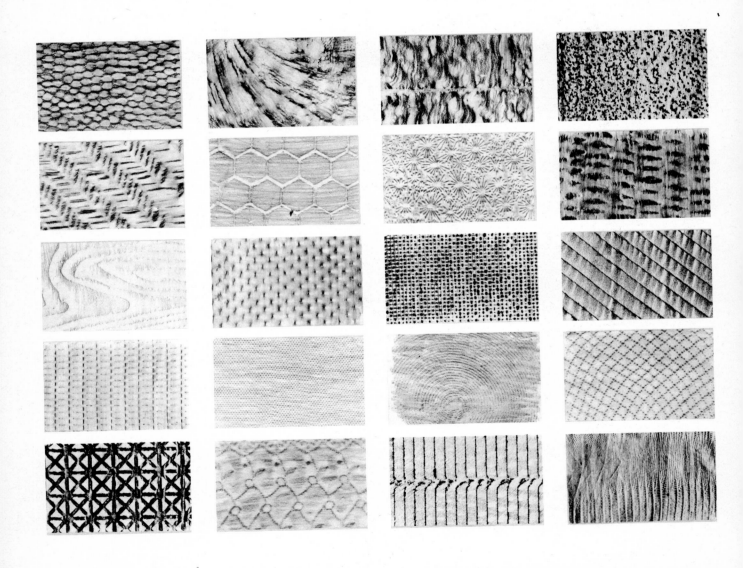

Drawing with Chalk

Procedure

1. *Light chalks on dark papers*
   This type of drawing is helpful in aiding the child to interpret subjects which are light in value, such as snowscapes, snowmen, polar bears, spring flowers. The chalk and dark paper produces good contrast in tone and brilliance of color.

2. *Chalk on grey paper*
   A middle-tone grey paper allows for good contrasts in both light and dark chalks. This contrast is developed most effectively if some of the paper is allowed to show through.

3. *Chalk on colored paper*
   Subtle and bold contrasts may be achieved, depending on the colors chosen.

Supplies

1. Chalks
2. Colored paper
3. Fixative, or clear plastic spray
4. Insect sprayer or atomizer for application of fixative over chalk

Shading with Chalk Dust

Supplies

1. Chalk
2. Flat, hard tool for scraping
3. Cotton, face tissue, or chalk applicator

Procedure

1. Scrape the tool along the side of the chalk sticks to produce dust. The dust particles from the chalk may be scraped directly onto areas of drawings done in other media. The cotton can be used to blend the dust in tonal passages which will enrich the original drawing.

NOTE: Chalk is easily smeared, and the completed drawing should have some protection. Commercially manufactured transparent sprays and fixatives are of some help, as is a home recipe to be found on page 246.

Wet Paper Chalk Drawing

Procedure

1. Draw over the damp paper with the chalk. The colors will generally be brighter and more exciting than those applied to dry paper. It is possible to use wet and dry techniques on one drawing by painting plain water over some areas prior to drawing. If the paper is not of fairly heavy stock, there is a danger of irregular wrinkling and curling.

   NOTE: Soaking chalk sticks for ten minutes in a strong solution of sugar water before use reduces the tendency to smear. Commercially manufactured transparent sprays and fixatives are of some help, as is a home recipe to be found on page 246.

Supplies

1. Colored chalks
2. Wet paper

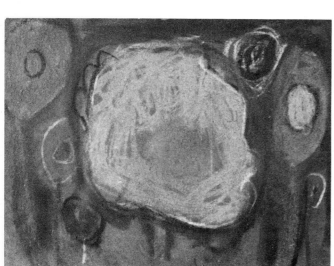

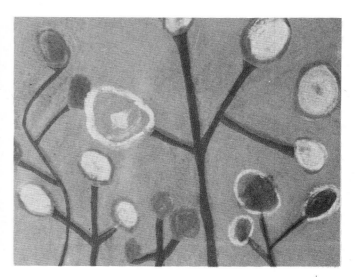

CRAFTS

Beads from Soda and Cornstarch Clay

Supplies

1. 1 cup cornstarch
2. 2 cups baking soda (1 lb. box)
3. 1¼ cups water
4. Saucepan
5. Stove or hot plate
6. Aluminum foil
7. Food coloring
8. Plastic bag
9. Watercolors or tempera paint
10. Clear commercial spray
11. Ball of clay (not necessary, but good for drying beads)—a piece of styrofoam could serve the same purpose
12. Toothpicks
13. Rolling pin or glass jar

Procedure

1. Combine the ingredients (1 cup cornstarch, 2 cups baking soda, 1¼ cup water) in a saucepan, and cook over medium heat, stirring constantly.
2. When the mixture is thickened to doughlike consistency, turn out on a piece of aluminum foil or breadboard.
3. Food coloring may be worked into the clay when it has cooled slightly.
4. Keep the clay in a refrigerator, covered with aluminum foil or plastic to keep it pliable when not in use.
5. Pinch off a lump of the mixture and shape into a bead. Spheres and cylinders can be formed easily by rolling the mixture between the palms of the hands.
6. Roll out the mixture flat with a rolling pin or glass jar and cut flat beads from it.
7. Punch a hole through each bead with a toothpick. Leave the toothpicks in the beads and stick them into the ball of clay for drying. Turn the toothpicks in the beads occasionally to keep them from sticking.
8. Shellac the beads and, when they are dry, string them.

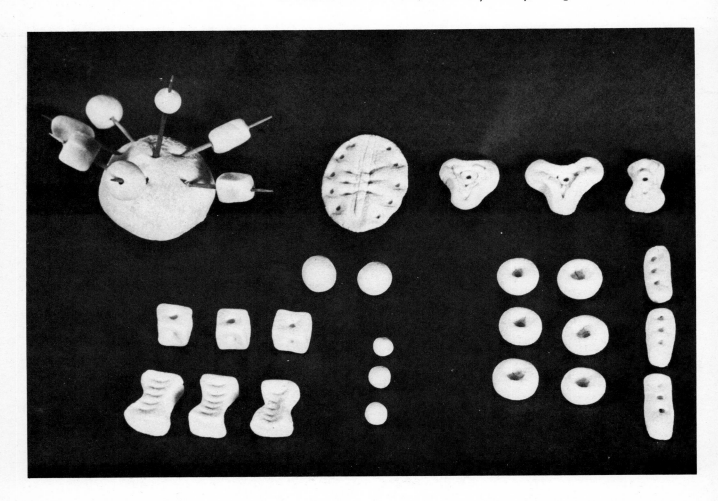

Cardboard Bracelets

Procedure

1. Cut cardboard tube into rings.
2. If tube will not fit over hand, cut out a section so that it will slip over the hand.
3. Wrap each ring with contact paper.
4. If contact paper is not available, cover the ring with tissue paper that has been soaked in a solution of starch or diluted paste.
5. Decorate with paint.
6. Spray with clear spray.

NOTE: String and other materials may be glued to the bracelet before finishing.

Supplies

1. Cardboard tube
2. Contact paper or tissue paper
3. Starch or paste
4. Tempera, or latex paint
5. Brush
6. Clear spray

Collage

A collage is similar to collé except that materials of all kinds are admissible to the picture. Painted and drawn passages may be combined with scrap materials to create a desired effect.

Supplies

1. Piece of cardboard
2. A collection of items most of which might be discarded (small scraps of cloth and textured paper, bottle caps, buttons, toothpicks, sand, pebbles, soda straws, string, yarn, rope, used sandpaper, etc.). Use only those items that can be adhered with some permanency to the cardboard.
3. Scissors
4. Paste or glue

Procedure

1. Arrange these items into a design or picture.
2. When satisfied, paste or glue on the cardboard background.
3. Any necessary details can be added with crayons or paints.

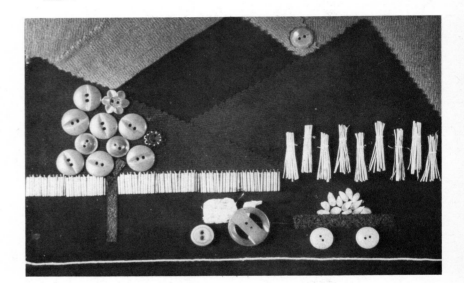

Eatable Cookies

Procedure

1. Cookie recipe:

   4 cups sifted flour
   2 teaspoons baking powder
   ¾ cups butter or margarine
     (1½ sticks)
   1½ cups sugar
   1 teaspoon salt
   2 eggs
   2 teaspoons vanilla
   1 teaspoon lemon extract

   Cookie paint:

   5 egg yolks
   2 teaspoons water
   food coloring

2. Sift flour, baking powder and salt into one bowl.
3. In second bowl, beat butter with sugar until light and fluffy.
4. Beat in eggs, vanilla, and lemon extract.
5. Stir in approximately one-third of flour mixture at a time.
6. Repeat until a stiff dough results.
7. Moisten table top and cover with wax paper (moisture will keep paper from slipping).
8. Roll out a portion of dough on the wax paper to a thickness of ¼ inch (Ill. 1).
9. Cut out desired shapes with sharp knife and trim away excess dough (Ill. 2). Cardboard patterns previously cut can be used.
10. Transfer cut cookies with pancake turner to lightly greased cookie sheet.
11. Repeat process with remaining dough.
12. To make cookie paint colors, beat egg yolks with water in bowl.
13. Divide egg yolk mixture into fruit glasses, one glass for each color to be used.
14. Add several drops of various food colors into each glass until desired color is obtained.
15. With a small brush, decorate each cookie. Make sure the paint is spread thickly to prevent cracking during baking (Ill. 3).
16. Place cookie sheet into moderate oven (375°) and bake cookies for ten minutes, or until dough is firm and light golden in color in unpainted areas.
17. Move cookies to wire rack until cool.

Supplies

1. Wax paper
2. Rolling pin
3. Sharply pointed knife
4. Small brush
5. Cookie sheet
6. Wire rack
7. Pancake turner
8. Three large bowls
9. Four or five small fruit glasses for cookie paint
10. Recipe

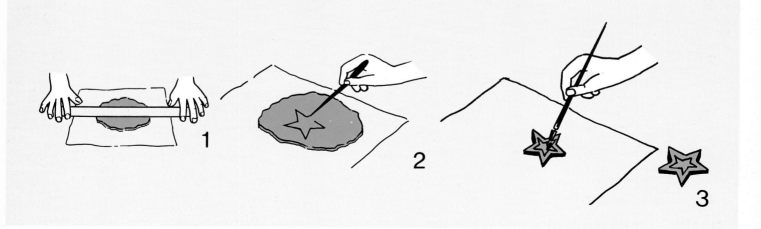

Embossed Metal

Supplies

1. Copper, aluminum, or brass foil
2. Modeling tool (anything that will not cut through or scratch the metal, such as spoon, pencil, sharpened wooden dowel, etc.)
3. Fine steel wool
4. Pencil and paper
5. Pad of newspaper or cloth (a turkish towel is excellent)
6. Oxidizing liquid (ammonium sulphide—a very unpleasant odor is produced, and adequate ventilation is recommended)
7. Clear plastic spray or lacquer (not necessary for aluminum)

Procedure

1. Cut the foil to the size of the finished work.
2. Develop a design on paper, the same size as the piece of foil.
3. Place the drawing on the foil and transfer the design by retracing the line with a pencil, pressing hard enough to make an impression.
4. Place the foil on a pad of newspaper or cloth. Decide which areas of the design are to be raised, and with a suitable tool (large, small, pointed, etc.) begin to press the foil into shape. Emboss the foil from both sides to avoid crinkling the metal. Remove the pad, place on a smooth hard surface, and work around the raised portions to flatten the background.
5. Copper foil can be oxidized by painting the design with ammonium sulphide until the entire surface is darkened. Wash the foil under running water and dry it.
6. Clean and polish the foil with steel wool. The oxidizing will remain in the low areas.
7. Lacquer or clear plastic spray applied to the copper or brass foil will keep it from tarnishing.

NOTE: Numerous textures can be embossed to give richness to the modeling. Enamel or lacquer will adhere to the foil to add color.

Gesso Plate

Procedure

1. Mix the gesso according to the directions on the can, or see formula page 245.
2. Paint two or three paper plates on both sides with the gesso, which should be the consistency of heavy cream.
3. Press the plates together while still wet, making sure the edges fit tightly. Allow them to dry.
4. Apply as many coats of gesso as are necessary to fill any cracks or nicks, or to produce the desired thickness. Allow this to dry.
5. Sandpaper the plate until smooth.
6. Paint the entire plate with a base color.
7. Decorations can now be added with contrasting colors.
8. Apply a protective coat of varnish, shellac, or plastic spray over the plate if tempera paint is used.

Supplies

1. Commercial dry ground gesso (or see formula on page 245)
2. Hot plate and old double boiler
3. Paper plates
4. Shellac, varnish, or clear plastic spray
5. Brush
6. Tempera paint or enamel paint

Linear String

Supplies

1. Heavy string or cord
2. Wax paper
3. Glue
4. Pencil
5. Paper
6. Tape

Procedure

1. Make pencil drawing of the desired subject.
2. Cover the pencil drawing with wax paper and fasten it in place with tape.
3. Place glue-covered string on wax paper over the line drawing.
4. When glue is dry, remove the string construction from the wax paper.

NOTE: If color is wanted, the string can be dyed before or painted after the design is completed. These objects should be incorporated into mobiles.

Mosaic Plaster Plaque

Procedure

1. Place the container which is to be used as a mold on a sheet of paper and trace around it with a pencil. This will provide a pictorial area of the same dimensions as the completed work, on which the preliminary drawing may be done. Divide the subject matter in the drawing into interesting sections which can be easily cut from the linoleum or plastic tile.

2. Transfer the various parts of the design to the linoleum or floor tile of the desired color and cut out with scissors. Break into pieces with the pliers if brittle plastic is used.

3. Place a small spot of paste on the face of each piece and fasten face down in the cardboard mold to form the original design. Approximately one-eighth of an inch space should remain between the various sections and the edge of the mold.

4. Mix the plaster as follows (see illustrations, pages 66 and 67):
   a. Pour the desired amount of water in the mixing container.
   b. Add the plaster to the water by sifting it through the fingers or gently shaking it from a can or small cup.
   c. Continue adding the sifted plaster to the water until the plaster builds up above the surface.
   d. Stir the plaster thoroughly with the hands until it is smooth and creamy, making sure that any lumps of plaster are broken. Stir gently to avoid bubbles.
   e. Once the plaster is mixed do not add more water to thin, or more plaster to thicken, because the same consistency cannot be regained.

Supplies

1. Cardboard container to be used as a mold
2. Scraps of thin colored or textured linoleum, or thin plastic floor tile
3. Molding plaster
4. Bowl in which to mix plaster
5. Heavyduty scissors
6. Paste
7. Pliers

5. Pour the plaster into the mold to the desired thickness. Agitate the box gently to make sure the plaster completely surrounds the individual pieces of the design and to also bring any bubbles to the surface. A wire hook can be placed in the plaster before it hardens completely if a wall plaque is desired.

NOTE: Begin to clean up immediately after pouring the plaster in the mold— it will harden rapidly once the chemical reaction takes place. Any excess plaster remaining should be wiped from the pan immediately and rolled in newspaper so that it might be disposed of more easily. Do not wash plaster down any drain. When cleaning the hands, tools, and mixing pan, be sure the water runs continuously.

6. Allow the plaster to dry thoroughly before removing the cardboard box mold. If the cardboard adheres to the plaster, wash it off under running water.
7. Smooth any of the sharp edges by scraping with any available tool. Repair any flaws that might appear at this time.
8. The finished plaque can be soaked in a solution of white soap flakes and then wiped dry with a cloth. This will produce a glossy and high-polish finish.

NOTE: A plaster relief can be created by carefully lifting out the pieces of plastic tile or linoleum.

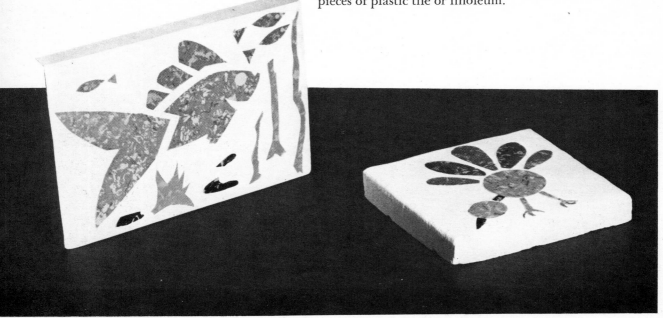

Papier-Mâché Bowl

Procedure

1. Cover the outside surface of the bowl with a film of cream, vaseline or grease. This will keep the papier-mâché from sticking to the bowl.
2. Place the bowl upside down on newspaper or cardboard.
3. Cut newspaper or paper toweling into strips, approximately one-half of an inch wide.
4. Mix the paste in a bowl or pan to the consistency of cream.
5. Place a strip of paper into the paste until it is saturated. Remove the strip from the bowl and wipe off the excess paste by pulling it between the fingers.
6. Apply the paste-saturated strips directly on the oiled surface of the bowl. One or two layers of strips of just-wet paper applied directly to the bowl before applying the paste-saturated strips will serve the same purpose as greasing bowl.

7. Continue to apply strips until the entire bowl is covered. Repeat until at least six layers of paper strips are applied. The number of layers can be readily counted if a different kind or color of paper is used for each layer. The strength of the finished bowl will be much greater if each layer of strips is applied in a different direction. Also, make sure that all wrinkles and bubbles are removed after each strip is added.
8. Allow the papier-mâché to dry thoroughly before removing the bowl.
9. Trim the edges of the bowl and apply additional strips to strengthen and smooth the edges. Other imperfections can be repaired at this time.
10. When thoroughly dry, sandpaper the surface until smooth and then decorate.
11. If tempera paint is used for decoration, the surface should be sprayed with clear plastic or painted with shellac or varnish for permanence.
12. Asphaltum painted on the inside of the bowl will waterproof the container.

Supplies

1. Newspapers, paper toweling, or any absorbent paper
2. Scissors or paper cutter
3. Paste thinned to the consistency of cream (wheat paste, library paste, etc.)
4. Container for mixing paste
5. A smooth bowl to be used as a mold. The bowl should also have a small base and a wide mouth with no undercuts.
6. Vaseline, grease, or cream
7. Sandpaper
8. Paint (tempera, enamel, oil paint, etc.)
9. Brush
10. Clear plastic spray, shellac or varnish for protective finish if tempera paint is used
11. Asphaltum to waterproof bowl

Papier-Mâché Jewelry

Supplies

1. Small pieces of styrofoam
2. Newspapers, paper toweling, or any absorbent paper
3. Scissors, or paper cutter
4. Paste thinned to consistency of cream
5. Container for mixing paste
6. Sandpaper
7. Paint (tempera, enamel, latex, etc.)
8. Brush
9. Clear plastic spray, shellac, or varnish for protecting finish, if tempera paint is used
10. Glue
11. Jewelry findings (pin and/or earring backs)

Procedure

1. Shape a piece of styrofoam to correspond identically to the desired piece of jewelry.
2. Cut newspaper or paper toweling into strips, approximately one-fourth of an inch wide.
3. Mix the paste in a bowl or pan to the consistency of cream.
4. Immerse a strip of paper into the paste until it is saturated. Remove the strip from the bowl and wipe off the excess paste by pulling it between the fingers.
5. Apply the strips directly to the styrofoam.
6. Continue to apply strips until the entire piece of jewelry is covered. Repeat until several layers of paper strips are applied. The number of layers can be readily counted if a different kind or color of paper is used for each layer. Make sure that all wrinkles and bubbles are removed after each strip is added.
7. Add any desired particular features. This can be done either with papier-mâché or by adding other materials.
8. Allow the papier-mâché to dry thoroughly.
9. Sandpaper the surface until smooth and then decorate.
10. If tempera paint is used for decoration, the surface should be sprayed with clear plastic or painted with shellac or varnish for permanence.
11. Fasten earring or pin back to the back of dry papier-mâché jewelry using glue mixed with a small piece of cotton.

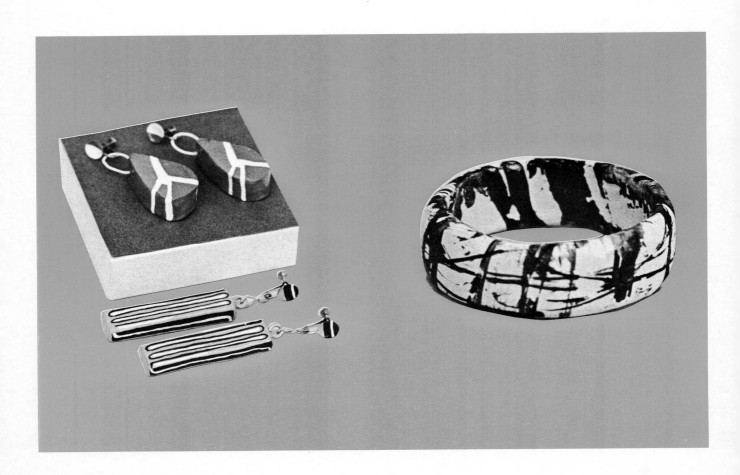

Papier-Mâché Maraca

Procedure

1. Cut newspaper or paper toweling into strips, approximately one-half of an inch wide.
2. Mix the paste in a bowl or pan to the consistency of cream.
3. Place a strip of paper into the paste until it is saturated. Remove the strip from the bowl and wipe off the excess paste by pulling it between the fingers.
4. Apply the paste-saturated strip directly to the light bulb.
5. Continue to apply strips until the entire bulb is covered. Repeat until at least six layers of paper strips are applied. The number of layers can be readily counted if a different kind or color of paper is used for each layer. The strength of the finished maraca will be much greater if each strip is applied in a different direction. Also, make sure that all wrinkles and bubbles are removed after each strip is added.
6. Place the maraca on a crumpled piece of newspaper, and allow to dry thoroughly. The crumpled paper allows the air to circulate around the maraca.
7. When completely dry, rap the maraca sharply against the floor, wall, or radiator to break the bulb inside the paper covering. The broken pieces of glass provides the sound when shaken. If a hole is punctured it is easily repaired with the addition of more strips.
8. Sandpaper the surface until smooth and then decorate.
9. If tempera paint is used for decoration the surface should be sprayed with clear plastic or painted with shellac or varnish for permanence.

Supplies

1. Newspapers, paper toweling, or any absorbent paper
2. Scissors, or paper cutter
3. Paste thinned to the consistency of cream
4. Container for mixing paste
5. Large burned-out electric light bulb
6. Sandpaper
7. Paint (tempera, enamel, oil paint, etc.)
8. Brush
9. Clear plastic spray, shellac, or varnish for protecting finish if tempera paint is used

Papier-Mâché over Balloon

Supplies

1. Newspapers, paper toweling or any absorbent paper
2. Scissors or paper cutter
3. Paste thinned to the consistency of cream (wheat paste, library paste, etc.)
4. Container for mixing paste
5. Balloon
6. Sandpaper
7. Paint (tempera, enamel, oil paint, etc.)
8. Brush
9. Clear plastic spray, shellac, or varnish for protective finish if tempera paint is used

Procedure

1. Cut newspaper or paper toweling into strips, approximately one-half of an inch wide.
2. Mix the paste in a bowl or pan to the consistency of cream.
3. Inflate the balloon to the desired size and tie it closed.
4. Place a strip of paper in the paste until it is saturated. Remove the strip from the bowl and wipe off the excess paste by pulling it between the fingers.
5. Apply the paste-saturated strip directly to the balloon.

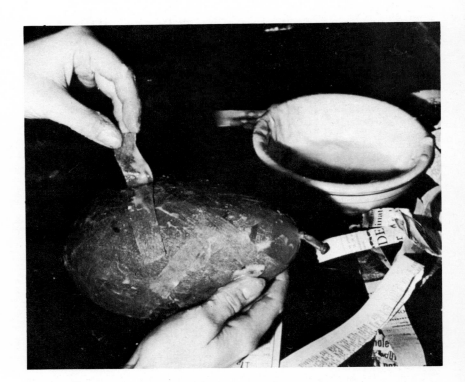

6. Continue to apply strips until the entire balloon is covered. Repeat until at least six layers of paper strips are applied. The number of layers can be readily counted if a different kind or color of paper is used for each layer. The strength of the finished balloon will be much greater if each strip is applied in a different direction. Also, make sure that all wrinkles and bubbles are removed after each strip is added.
7. Allow papier-mâché to dry thoroughly.
8. A number of different and interesting objects can be created at this point.

   a. An opening can be cut into an egg shape and an Easter egg crèche can be built inside.
   b. A perfect sphere can be used as a globe for the geography class. The continents can be painted, built up with papier-mâché, or built in relief with a salt and flour mixture. (See page 212.)
   c. When cut in half, the balloon shape can be used as a foundation for two masks, two bowls, or one of each. If a mask is desired, openings can be cut for the eyes, and features added with either

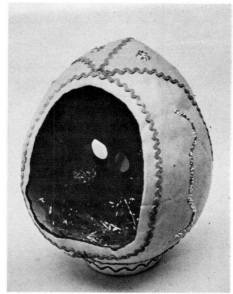

papier-mâché or by fastening other materials in place (yarn for hair, kernels of corn for teeth, cut paper for ears, etc.).

    d. The shape of the papier-mâché balloon might suggest an animal, bird, fish, etc. Its particular features can be applied with papier-mâché or by fastening other material to the form.

9. Sandpaper the surface of any of the above objects before decorating.
10. If tempera paint is used for decoration the surface should be sprayed with clear plastic or painted with shellac or varnish for permanence.

Papier-Mâché over Bottle

Supplies

1. Newspapers, paper toweling, or any absorbent paper
2. Scissors or paper cutter
3. Paste thinned to consistency of cream
4. Container for mixing paste
5. Bottle on which to build form
6. Sandpaper
7. Paint (tempera, latex, enamel, etc.)
8. Brush
9. Clear plastic spray, shellac, or varnish, for protecting finish if tempera paint is used

Procedure

1. Build a frame or armature to the general shape of the chosen subject. Fasten the various parts of the skeleton together securely, using the wire, nails, tape, or appropriate material.
2. Cut newpaper or paper toweling into strips, approximately one-half of an inch wide.
3. Mix the paste in a bowl or pan to the consistency of cream.
4. Place a strip of paper in the paste until it is saturated. Remove the strip from the bowl and wipe off the excess paste by pulling the strip between the fingers.
5. Apply the strips directly over the frame.
6. Continue to apply strips until the entire frame is covered. Repeat until at least six layers of paper strips are applied. The number of layers can be readily counted if a different kind or color of paper is used for each layer. The strength of the finished frame will much greater if each strip is applied in a different direction. Also, make sure that all wrinkles and bubbles are removed after each strip is added.
7. Add any particular features not incorporated in the original skeleton. This can be done either with papier-mâché or by adding other materials.
8. Allow the papier-mâché to dry thoroughly.
9. Sandpaper the surface until smooth and then decorate.
10. If tempera paint is used for decoration the surface should be sprayed with clear plastic or painted with shellac or varnish for permanence.
11. Additional materials such as yarn for hair, buttons for eyes, etc., can be added to further enhance the finished product.

Papier-Mâché over Frame

Procedure

1. Cut newspaper or paper toweling into strips, approximately one-half of an inch wide.
2. Mix the paste in a bowl or pan to the consistency of cream.
3. Submerge a strip of paper in the paste until it is saturated. Remove the strip from the bowl and wipe off the excess paste by pulling the strip between the fingers.
4. Apply the paste-saturated strip directly to the bottle.
5. Continue to apply strips until the entire bottle is covered. Repeat until at least six layers of paper strips are applied. The number of layers can be readily counted if a different kind or color of paper is used for each layer. The strength of the finished piece will be much greater if each strip is applied in a different direction. Also, make sure that all wrinkles and bubbles are removed after each strip is added.
6. Place the bottle on a crumpled piece of paper, and allow to dry thoroughly. The crumpled paper allows the air to circulate around the piece.
7. When the papier-mâché over the bottle is dry, the surface can be decorated with a choice of three-dimensional materials which are held in position with paste-covered strips.
8. When dry, sandpaper the surface until smooth, and then decorate.
9. If tempera paint is used for decoration the surface should be sprayed with clear plastic or painted with shellac or varnish for permanence.

Supplies

1. Window screen, chicken wire, wire, paper, mailing tubes, sticks, etc. (to be used individually or collectively to form the general shape of the object to be covered with papier-mâché)
2. Wire, nails, gummed paper, glue, etc., for use in fastening the frame together
3. Newspapers, paper toweling, or any absorbent paper
4. Scissors, or paper cutter
5. Paste thinned to the consistency of cream
6. Container for mixing paste
7. Sandpaper
8. Paint (tempera, enamel, oil paint, etc.)
9. Brush
10. Clear plastic spray, shellac, or varnish for protecting finish if tempera paint is used

Papier-Mâché Pulp Objects

Supplies

1. Newspaper, or tissue, or paper towels
2. Wallpaper paste
3. Table salt
4. Container

Procedure

1. Tear (do not cut with cutter or scissors) paper into small pieces no bigger than one-half inch square. Be sure edges of pieces are ragged.
2. Place the torn paper in a container and cover with water, and, at the same time, stir to make sure all the paper becomes wet.
3. Add a teaspoonful of salt for each quart of mixture to prevent spoilage. Allow to soak for at least thirty-six hours.
4. Mix and squeeze the mixture until it becomes pulp.
5. Mix in wallpaper paste in small amounts as needed.
6. Model the forms with the mixture.
7. Allow the pulp to dry thoroughly.
8. Sandpaper the surface until smooth and then decorate.
9. If tempera paint is used for decoration, the surface should be sprayed with clear plastic or painted with shellac or varnish for permanence.

NOTE: Papier-mâché pulp can be used for dishes, plaques, ornaments, puppets, marionettes, maps, etc.

Papier-Mâché Puppet Head

Supplies

1. Newspapers, paper toweling, or any absorbent paper
2. Scissors, or paper cutter
3. Paste thinned to the consistency of cream (wheat paste, library paste, etc.)
4. Container for mixing paste
5. Plastic clay
6. Sandpaper

Procedure

1. Create a puppet head and neck with the plastic clay. The neck will eventually serve two purposes: first, a place to fasten clothing, and secondly, a place for the middle finger to control the puppet. When forming the head exaggerate the features, as the thickness of the applied paper strips tends to reduce feature recognition.
2. Cut newspaper or paper toweling into strips, approximately one-half of an inch wide.
3. Mix the paste in a bowl or pan to the consistency of cream.
4. Place a strip of paper into the paste until it is saturated. Remove the

strip from the bowl and wipe off the excess paste by pulling the strip between the fingers.

5. Apply the paste-saturated strip directly to the puppet head.
6. Continue to apply strips until the entire head is covered. Repeat until at least six layers of paper strips are applied. The number of layers can be readily counted if a different kind or color of paper is used for each layer. The strength of the finished puppet will be much greater if each strip is applied in a different direction. Also, make sure that all wrinkles and bubbles are removed after each strip is added.
7. Place the puppet head on a crumpled piece of paper and allow it to dry thoroughly. The crumpled paper allows the air to circulate around the puppet head.
8. When the puppet head is dry, cut it in half with a sharp knife or saw, and remove the clay (Ill. 1).
9. Place the two halves together, and fasten with additional strips. It may also be necessary to apply several strips over the bottom edge of the neck for strength.
10. When thoroughly dry, sandpaper until smooth, and then decorate (Ill. 2).
11. If tempera paint is used for decoration the surface should be sprayed with clear plastic, or painted with shellac or varnish for permanence.
12. Additional material such as yarn for hair, buttons for eyes, etc., can be added to further enhance the finished product (Ill. 3).

7. Knife, saw, or single-edge razor blade
8. Paint (tempera, enamel, oil paint, etc.)
9. Brush
10. Clear plastic spray, shellac, or varnish for protective finish if tempera paint is used

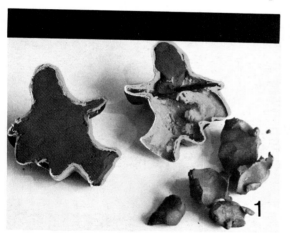

Pariscraft Figures

Supplies

1. A piece of cardboard to be used as a body, cut according to the desired size (a tube may be used)
2. Yarn, to be used as hair
3. Assorted fabrics
4. Glue
5. Cotton
6. Paints (acrylic recommended, tempera suitable)
7. Wheat paste (optional)
8. Pariscraft (fabric, in roll, with pre-applied coating of plaster)

Procedure

1. Roll up the cardboard to produce a cone. Staple or glue the ends together. Cut off the point.
2. Tear off a piece of cotton the size desired for the head.
3. Cut Pariscraft into small strips which can be dampened and wrapped around the cotton ball.
4. When dry, glue the head on the narrow end of the cone.
5. Cut fairly long strips of Pariscraft to a width suitable for arms, and roll them up until the desired arm thickness is achieved. Cut the roll in half and dampen.
6. Glue the arms to the cone (body).
7. Glue the pieces of yarn to the head, building it up to simulate hair. If desired, the yarn may first be dipped in wheat paste, in which case the glue is unnecessary.
8. Paint the face, its features, and the arms.
9. Produce the desired clothed effect by painting and/or gluing material to the body.

NOTE: This procedure describes a method of making small figures; experimentation will reveal many other possibilities.

Peep Box

Procedure

As in the shadowbox (page 77), the procedure for this project will vary somewhat, depending upon the type of peep box to be made. Scenes from children's stories, poems, or songs may be depicted in the peep boxes. It is possible, too, to create make-believe aquariums (suspend the fish, etc., from a string and use colored cellophane over the top and face of the box to give the illusion of water). Peep boxes can also be very effective as Christmas crèches and puppet theaters.

1. Cut a small spy-hole opening in one end of a box. In some cases an opening at each end is advisable.
2. Cut a number of openings or doors in the lid in order to allow light in the box. These openings can be placed strategically to allow spot-lighting. Light can be controlled in the box by opening or closing the "doors" in the lid.
3. Design the sides of the box. Any one of a number of techniques may be used for this: potato print, crayon engraving, chalk stencil, colored paper, finger paint, water color, etc. A combination of several of these techniques will make an interesting peep box.
4. Many methods are available for making trees, houses, barns, figures, etc. Cleansing tissue can be modeled as the foliage for trees. It may be tinted with colored inks or tempera paint. Twigs, match sticks and paper cylinders can serve as the trunks of the tree. Bits of sponges also make suitable foliage when painted. One may choose to use paper sculpture as a method of making trees, schrubs, etc.

   Houses, barns, and other buildings can be made from tiny boxes, corrugated cardboard , or paper sculpture. These, too, may be painted with colored inks or tempera paints.

   Figures and animals can be made from wire, pipe cleaners, clay, salt and flour mixture, papier-mâché, clothes pins, etc.

Supplies

1. Cardboard box (shoe box, hat box, etc.)
2. Scissors
3. Rubber cement, paste, glue, or stapler
4. Tempera paint, watercolors, crayons, colored chalks, or color inks
5. Paint brush and water jar, if paints are used
6. Assorted papers
7. A variety of materials to be used for decorative purposes, cloth, felt, ribbon, yarn, dried coffee grounds, buttons, clay, salt and flour mixture, twigs, pebbles, etc. These materials can be determined more easily after the subject for the peep box has been decided upon.

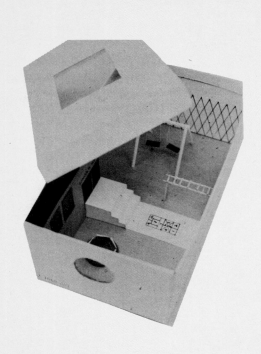

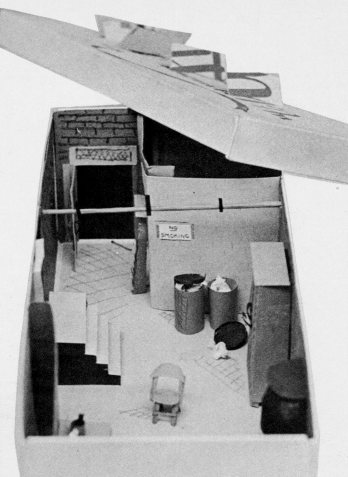

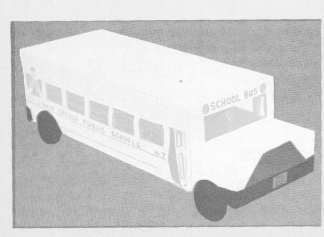

Pipe Cleaner Figures

Procedure

1. Interesting stick figures can be created by bending and twisting the pipe cleaners.
2. Form and thickness can be added to the stick figures by wrapping additional pipe cleaners around the body, arms, and legs, etc.

   NOTE: These figures may be used in shadowboxes, sand table displays, small stage sets, or for individual party favors or decorations.

Supplies

1. White or colored pipe cleaners
2. Any cutting tool which can be used to cut the pipe cleaners to the desired length

Plaster Mixing

Supplies

1. Molding plaster
2. Container for mixing plaster
3. Water
4. Newspaper for cleaning
5. Container to be used as mold

Procedure

Mix the plaster as follows:

1. Pour the desired amount of water into the mixing container.
2. Add the plaster to the water by sifting it through the fingers or gently shaking it from a can or small cup.
3. Continue adding the sifted plaster to the water until the plaster builds up above the surface. Allow to soak twenty or thirty seconds to thoroughly blend the mixture.
4. Stir the plaster thoroughly with the hands until it is smooth and creamy, making sure that any lumps of plaster are broken, and stir gently to avoid bubbles.
5. Once the plaster is mixed do not add more water to thin, or more plaster to thicken, because the same consistency cannot be regained.
6. Pour the plaster into a container which can be used for the mold. Agitate the mold gently to bring any bubbles to the surface.

NOTE: Begin to clean up immediately after pouring the plaster in the mold—it will harden rapidly once the chemical reaction takes place. Any excess plaster remaining should be wiped from the pan immediately and rolled in newspaper so that it might be disposed of more easily. Do not wash plaster down any drain. When cleaning the hands, tools, and mixing pan, be sure the water runs continuously.

Plaster Space Forms

Supplies

1. Plaster
2. Small balloon
3. Yarn
4. Bowl for mixing plaster
5. Can of spray paint, if color is desired

Procedure

1. Inflate the balloon and tie the end closed.
2. Mix plaster as follows (see illustrations pages 66 and 67):
   a. Pour the desired amount of water in the mixing container.
   b. Add the plaster to the water by sifting it through the fingers or gently shaking it from a can or small cup.
   c. Continue adding the sifted plaster to the water until the plaster builds up above the surface.
   d. Stir the plaster thoroughly with the hands until it is smooth and creamy, making sure that any lumps of plaster are broken and stir gently to avoid bubbles.
   e. Once the plaster is mixed do not add more water to thin, or more plaster to thicken, because the same consistency cannot be regained.
3. Holding one end of the yarn, immerse it in the plaster (if the yarn is too fine, use a double or triple strand). Pull the yarn from the bowl, and through the fingers of one hand, wiping off the excess plaster.
4. Place the plaster-saturated yarn on the inflated balloon in a decorative manner, making sure the yarn crosses over itself frequently.

NOTE: Begin to clean up when the plaster begins to thicken—it will harden rapidly once the chemical reaction takes place. Any excess plaster remaining should be wiped from the pan immediately and rolled in newspaper so that it might be disposed of more easily. Do not wash plaster down any drain. When cleaning hands, tools, and mixing pan, be sure the water runs continuously.

5. Allow the plaster to harden and dry thoroughly before puncturing the balloon.
6. Hold the plaster-decorated balloon in a wastebasket, or large cardboard box to catch the numerous plaster chips that result when the balloon is punctured.
7. Gently smooth any rough edges and paint the plaster. Spray paint will work best. Painting before the balloon is punctured will leave the inside pure white.
8. Additional decoration of various materials can be placed inside the space form.

Plaster Tile Mosaic

Procedure

1. Place the wood or masonite to be used as the tile on a sheet of paper and trace around it with a pencil. This will provide a pictorial area the same dimensions as the completed tile.
2. Create a drawing within this area.
3. Transfer the drawing to the wood or masonite.
4. Break the plastic into small pieces with the pliers and glue in place on the tile. Allow a small space between each piece as it is placed. If pieces are too small they can be picked up with tweezers.

   a. Avoid light-colored tiles as they will not contrast with the white plaster surrounding each piece.
   b. If the entire tile is not to be covered with mosaic, be sure a border is included.

5. Mix the plaster as follows (see illustrations, pages 66 and 67):

   a. Pour the desired amount of water into the mixing container.
   b. Add the plaster to the water by sifting it through the fingers, or gently shaking it from a can or small cup.
   c. Continue adding the sifted plaster to the water until the plaster builds up above the surface of the water.
   d. Stir the plaster thoroughly with the hands until it is smooth and creamy. Make sure any lumps of plaster are broken and also stir gently to avoid creating bubbles.
   e. Once the plaster is mixed, do not add any more water to thin, or more plaster to thicken, because the same consistency cannot be regained.

6. Pour the plaster over the tile which has been placed on newspaper and work it between the mosaic pieces.

   NOTE: Begin to clean up immediately after pouring the plaster into the mold—it will harden rapidly once the chemical reaction takes place. Any excess plaster remaining should be wiped from the pan immediately and rolled in newspaper so that it might be disposed of more easily. Do not wash plaster down any drain. When cleaning the hands, tools, and mixing pan, be sure the water runs continuously.

7. Level the plaster by pulling the straightedge over the surface. (Thin pieces of mosaic should be used, as thick pieces will be pulled out of place.)
8. Fill in all bubbles and repair any flaws before the plaster becomes too hard.
9. Only a thin film of plaster should appear on the mosaic tiles after scraping with the straightedge.
10. When almost dry, clean film from the tile pieces with fingers, tissue or rag.

Supplies

1. Piece of wood or masonite the size of the mosaic to be made
2. Scraps of thin colored plastic floor tile (all must be the same thickness)
3. Molding plaster
4. Bowl in which to mix plaster
5. Pliers
6. Glue
7. Straightedge wider and longer than the tile to be made
8. Tweezers

Plastic Container Masks

Supplies

1. Empty gallon-size plastic container
2. Saw, scissors, or knife
3. Spray paint
4. Elastic to hold mask in place

Procedure

1. Cut empty container in half—each piece will serve as a mask. If possible, have the containers cut in half with a power band saw. Observe all safety precautions in using cutting tools.
2. Cut out any openings necessary for eyes, nose or mouth.
3. Additions can be added with pieces cut from the bottle or paper, paint and pipe cleaners.
4. Staple an elastic band to each side of the mask to hold it to the head comfortably.

NOTE: Empty containers can also be used for carryalls, planters and bird feeders. If planter is to be made from plastic container, stones should be placed in the bottom for drainage. Decoration can be added to the bird feeder with adhesive paper or paint.

Pressed Nature Notepaper

Procedure

1. Collect flowers, ferns, leaves, grasses, etc., and dry them by pressing between sheets of newspaper weighted with books or other heavy objects. Let them dry about one week, changing newspapers occasionally.
2. Arrange these natural objects where they appear to be most pleasing on the notepaper or place cards.
3. When satisfied with the arrangement, glue into place by dotting the backs of the leaves, flowers, etc., with glue, just enough to hold them in place until the Contact paper can be applied.
4. Cut a square or rectangle of clear Contact paper large enough to cover and extend a little beyond the design.
5. Peel the backing from the Contact paper and carefully apply it, pressing it firmly to the place card or notepaper. If a bubble forms in the Contact paper, prick it with a pin and press it out.

Supplies

1. Notepaper or place cards
2. Leaves, delicate flowers, lacy ferns, grasses, etc.
3. Newspapers
4. Glue
5. Clear Contact paper
6. Ruler
7. Scissors

Pressed Nature Picture

Supplies

1. Leaves, delicate flowers, lacy ferns, grasses, etc.
2. Newspapers
3. Matboard and cardboard the same size for backing
4. White or light-colored material (material used for drapery or dress linings is good)
5. Scissors
6. Ruler
7. Pencil
8. Razor blade
9. Glue
10. Decorative braids (optional)
11. Material to cover top mat (tiny checks or prints might enhance picture)
12. Inexpensive picture frame
13. Double-edged tape if mat is to be covered with material

Procedure

1. Collect flowers, leaves, ferns, grasses, etc., and dry them by pressing between sheets of newspaper weighted with books or other heavy objects. Let dry about one week, changing newspapers occasionally.
2. Follow steps one through nine on pages 114 and 115, "Matting Pictures," to determine the size of the finished picture.
3. White or light plain material may be stretched over the cardboard covering an area an inch larger all around than the opening of the mat.
4. Arrange dry, pressed flowers, leaves, etc., into a pleasing design and, when satisfied, glue them into place. (Just dot the backs of leaves, flowers, etc., with glue as they are pressed into place on the picture.)
5. The top mat of the picture may be covered with decorative material if desired. Stretch and turn the under-edge of the material and hold it in place with double-edged tape. The inside corners of the material will need to be slit in order to turn and tape. Simple, decorative braids, outlining the inside edge of mat, may enhance picture. It is necessary to experiment to obtain best results.
6. Frame the finished picture. (Frames may be spray painted, stained, or rubbed with gold paint and then buffed.)

Relief Mosaic from Seeds or Beads

Procedure

1. Sketch the design on construction paper, carefully defining the areas where seeds are to be placed.
2. Using glue, mount the construction paper on cardboard, the same size as the construction paper.
3. Spread the glue on one area of the design at a time and press the seeds, beads or natural objects into place, filling the area. (For a neater appearance in the design, it is best to outline each area, then proceed to fill the rest of the area.)
4. When placing small pieces, it is helpful to put a dab of glue on the end of a toothpick to pick up and place each seed.
5. When glue is completely dry and excess pieces have been shaken off, spray the design with three thin coats of clear spray.

NOTE: Additional details may be added to the picture with heavy string, yarn or other decorative materials (for whiskers, stems, etc.).

Supplies

1. Cardboard
2. Construction paper
3. White glue
4. Assortment of seeds or natural objects
5. Food coloring
6. Pencil
7. String or yarn
8. Clear spray

Salt and Flour Relief

Supplies

1. Combine three parts salt with one part flour, and enough water to bring solution to the consistency of dough. This will create a mass suitable for sculptural modeling; the thickness may be modified for individual needs or desired methods of application by varying the quantity of water.
2. Heavy cardboard or piece of wood
3. Watercolor paints
4. Brush
5. Water container

Procedure

1. Cover the cardboard or wood with a thin film of salt and flour mixture.
2. Keeping a design in mind, create a semi-round relief, building up masses of the salt and flour mixture to various heights. Additional salt and flour may be added when the first application has dried enough to support another layer.
3. When the modeling is completed, it may be embellished by the addition of color while still moist.
4. Additional interest may be created by pressing objects, textures, and patterns into the wet salt and flour.

NOTE: Topographical maps or aerial views are especially suitable for treatment in this manner.

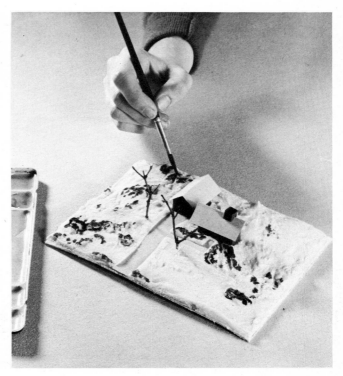

Sand Painting

Procedure

1. Sketch a design lightly with a pencil on the cardboard or wood.
2. Brush in the background colors in which sand is not desired.
3. Choose the areas to be done in a particular color sand and paint a thin coat of shellac, varnish, glue, or paste on these parts (paint a small area at a time).
4. Trickle or sprinkle the colored sand from a paper cone or spoon onto the areas that have been covered with paste, varnish, or shellac.
5. Allow the work to dry for a few minutes, then lift the work and tap it lightly so excess sand is removed.
6. Repeat this process for all additional colors.

NOTE: American Indians poured sand from the hand along the second joint of the index finger. The thumb was used to stop the flow of sand.

Supplies

1. Fine sand of various colors
2. Jars or bowls for mixing and storing the sand
3. Heavy cardboard or piece of wood
4. Paper cone or spoon
5. Varnish, shellac, glue, or paste
6. Watercolor paint
7. Brush

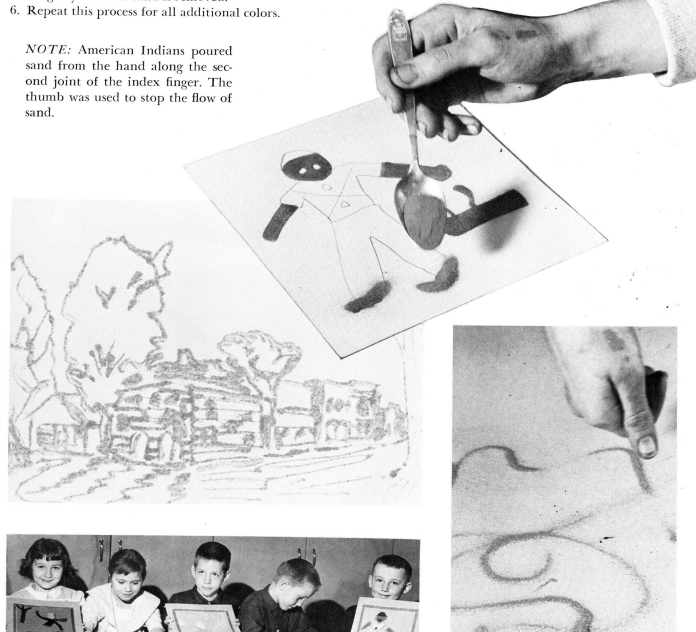

Sealed Nature Pattern

Supplies

1. Interesting forms of *flat* plant life, such as leaves, weeds, grasses
2. Wax paper
3. Iron

Procedure

1. Cut two sheets of wax paper which are of equal size.
2. Lay one sheet flat and arrange the plant life on it to create the desired pattern.
3. Place the other waxed sheet over the first, covering the plant life.
4. Iron over the second sheet with a *warm* flat iron. This will seal the waxed sheets together, preserving the plant life.

NOTE: Suggested applications for this design are: table runner, bulletin or blackboard frieze, window transparencies, etc.

Shadowbox

Procedure

The procedure for this project will vary somewhat, depending upon the type of shadowbox to be made. Scenes from children's stories, poems, or songs may be depicted in a shadowbox. It is possible, too, to create make-believe aquariums (suspend the fish, etc., from a string and use colored cellophane over the face of the box to give the illusion of water). Shadowboxes can also be very effective as Christmas crèches and puppet theaters.

1. Design the background for the picture. Any one of a number of techniques may be used for this: potato printing, crayon engraving, chalk stenciling, finger painting, watercolor, etc. A combination of several of these techniques will make an interesting background for the shadowbox.

2. Many methods are available for making trees, houses, barns, figures, etc. Cleansing tissue can be modeled into the foliage for trees. It may be tinted with colored inks or tempera paint. Twigs, match sticks, or paper cylinders can serve as the trunks of the tree. Bits of sponges also make suitable foliage when painted. One may choose to use paper sculpture as a method of making trees, shrubs, etc.

   Houses, barns, and other buildings can be made from tiny boxes, corrugated cardboard, or paper sculpture. These, too, may be painted with colored inks or tempera paints.

   Figures and animals can be made from wire, pipe cleaners, clay, the salt and flour mixture, papier-mâché, clothes pins, etc.

NOTE: The possibilities for this project are unlimited. The methods and materials should be left to the discretion of the teacher, according to the age and capacities of the pupils making the shadowboxes.

Supplies

1. Cardboard box (shoe box, hat box, etc.)
2. Scissors
3. Rubber cement, paste, glue, or stapler
4. Tempera paint, watercolors, crayons, colored chalks, or colored inks
5. Paint brush and water jar, if paints are used
6. Assorted papers
7. A variety of materials to be used for decorative purposes—cloth, felt, ribbon, yarn, dried coffee grounds, buttons, clay, salt and flour mixture, twigs, pebbles, etc. These materials can be determined more easily after the subject for the shadowbox has been decided upon.

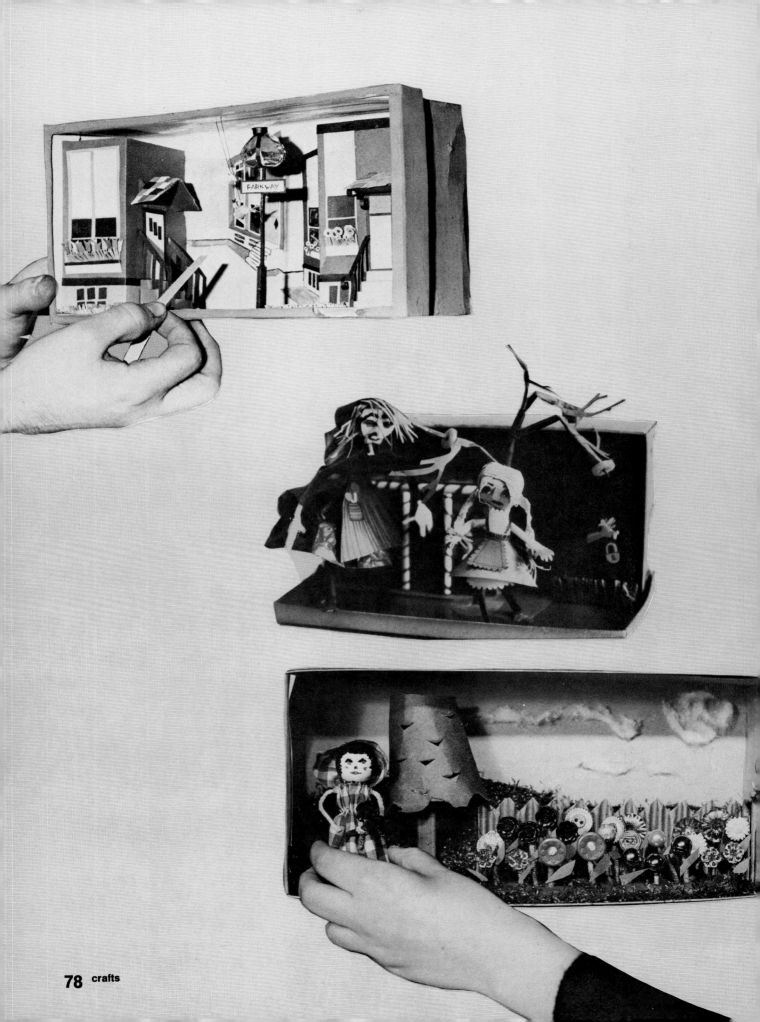

String Picture

Procedure

1. Make a light pencil drawing on a sheet of paper. Use colored paper if white string is to be used.
2. Coat the string with glue, then place it over the pencil lines.

   NOTE: When using yarn, it may be easier to trail the glue on the drawing and place the yarn on the glue.

Supplies

1. String or yarn
2. Paper
3. Glue

String and Pin Plaques

Supplies

1. Upsom board, ½ inch thick
2. Straight pins
3. Assorted colors of thread or string
4. Piece of felt or cloth
5. Tape or glue

Procedure

1. Decide on size and shape of plaque and cut from a piece of Upsom Board.
2. Cover Upsom Board with a piece of felt or cloth. Pull the cloth over the edges and fasten in back with glue or tape. Be sure cloth is stretched tightly.
3. Push enough straight pins into cloth-covered Upsom Board to form a design. Measure the distance between the pins if the design is to be geometric.
4. Tie string or thread to one pin, then wind around other pins to form design.
5. Tie string when one color design is completed. Tie another color string to a pin, and begin to form another part of design.
6. Place hook in back so plaque may be hung.

Sucker Stick Construction

Procedure

A. 1. First, cut the wooden pieces for the back and front of the structure. (The hole for a wren house should be one inch in diameter.)
   2. Sucker sticks are then glued to the edges of the front and back pieces to enclose the shape.

B. 1. Various bowls or other constructions can be created by laying sticks on top of one another much like laying bricks. Place a drop of glue where sticks cross one another.
   2. Continue process until bowl is built to desired height.

   NOTE: Various combinations of sucker sticks may be used to create figures, creatures or objects.

Supplies

1. Sucker sticks
2. Fine sandpaper
3. Glue
4. Enamel spray paint or fast drying clear finish
5. Wooden pieces for back and front of structure

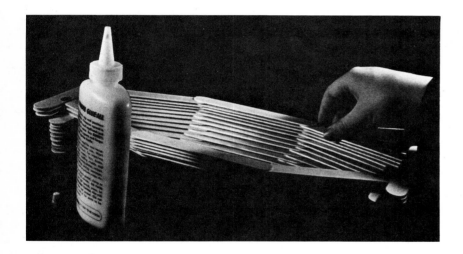

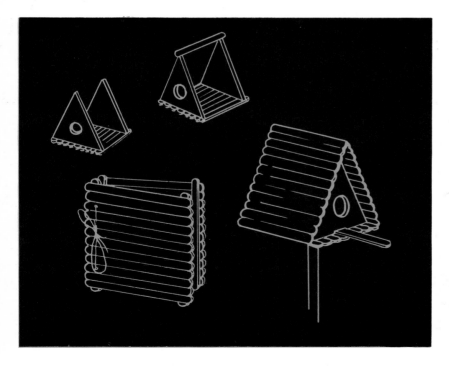

CRAYON

Nature of the Medium

Crayons

Of the many art materials, probably none is more familiar than wax crayons. The fact that most of us were introduced to them at a tender age may influence us to think that they are beneath the dignity of more mature artists. Such is not the case; examples abound of distinguished drawings executed in this humble medium, although few can be dated before the nineteenth century.

Crayons consist of an oily or waxy binder impregnated with pigments. Records exist of a variety of prescriptions for binders, involving soap, salad oil, linseed oil, spermaceti and beeswax. Crayons are of various types, some soft, some semi-hard; some are specifically designed for lithographic work, others for general classroom use.

Crayons work well on most papers. They do not blend well; when attempts are made to do this, the wax often "tears." Thus, most drawings are linear in character. Crayons can be scraped thin to produce semi-transparent layers of subtle color, and they can be coated with black and scratched through, for crayon etchings.

This is an ideal medium for children; it is bold, colorful, clean and inexpensive.

Crayon Etching

Procedure

1. Cover the entire surface of the paper with a heavy coat of brightly colored crayons in either a free or a planned design. Avoid using dark colors. The heavier the colors are applied the better the final result. No definite drawing or design is necessary at this point.
2. Crayon over the brightly colored crayoned surface with black, violet, or any dark color, until no original color shows. Rubbing the crayon-covered surface with a piece of tissue or cloth first will help the dark crayon adhere.
3. Having a definite design or drawing in mind, scratch or scrape through the dark surface to the color or colors beneath.

Supplies

1. Wax crayons
2. Drawing paper (white or manila)
3. Scraping tool (scissors, stick, hairpin, comb, nail, nail file, etc.)

Crayon Doodle Designs

Supplies

1. Paper
2. Pencil
3. Crayons or paint

Procedure

1. Cover the entire area of the paper with a continuous line drawn with complete spontaneity in light pencil. Make sure this line contains numerous directions made by a variety of straight and curved lines.
2. Look for shapes that are created by the lines and draw them in with a heavy pencil line. Many interesting abstract designs, as well as subject matter, can be found.
3. Crayon or paint the finished picture.

NOTE: The top doodle was the beginning of each drawing below it. Arrows indicate the starting points of the doodles.

Crayon on Cloth

Procedure

1. Draw directly on the cloth with the crayons, using considerable pressure.
2. Melt the crayon into the cloth by placing it under a heat lamp or ironing over it between sheets of paper.

   NOTE: The color will be semi-permanent only if the fabric is washed in *cool* water with a *nondetergent* soap.

Supplies

1. Wax crayons
2. Heat lamp or hot iron
3. Cotton fabric, which must be washed thoroughly to cleanse it of all sizing or stiffener

Crayon over Tempera Paint

Supplies

1. Tempera paints and brush
2. Wax crayons
3. Paper
4. Sponge

Procedure

1. Create the desired painting with tempera paints.
2. Work a contrasting color over each area with crayon, using moderate pressure.
3. Immerse the sponge in water; then "wash" the painting until the underlying tempera paint begins flaking off. The result will be a mottled, textured quality in which the residual crayon will supplement and accent the varied tempera tones which remain. The degree of flaking may be accelerated by brushing or, if it has gone too far, retouching may be done with the crayon.

NOTE: This procedure may be modified by applying the crayons more heavily, then holding the drawing under water which is just hot enough to melt them. The use of hot water necessitates a degree of caution. Perhaps the teacher would elect to perform this phase of the problem for each child.

Crayon Resist

Procedure

1. Color drawing or design heavily with crayons, allowing areas of paper to show.
2. Cover the entire surface of the paper with watercolor paint. The paint will be absorbed by the uncolored paper and resisted by the wax crayons.

   NOTE: If light-colored or white crayons are used, a dark watercolor wash will be most satisfactory.

Supplies

1. Wax crayon
2. Paper
3. Brush
4. Watercolor paints
5. Water container

Crayon Resist Batik

Supplies

1. Crayons
2. Manila paper
3. Pencil
4. Watercolors
5. Brush

Procedure

1. Make a light drawing in pencil on manila or heavy wrapping paper.
2. Using the pencil lines as a guide, draw lines and shapes with the crayon, allowing areas of the paper to show through.
3. Soak paper in water and crumple into a ball.
4. Uncrumple the paper, flatten and blot off excess water.
5. Paint the entire surface with watercolor paint or diluted tempera paint. The paint will be absorbed by the uncolored paper and resisted by the wax crayon, creating a weblike or batik pattern.

Crayon Rubbing

Procedure

1. Make an outline drawing or design with pencil on thin drawing paper.
2. Hold the drawing against a surface which has a definite texture and rub the crayon over all areas of the drawing in which the texture will create a pleasing pattern. The texture will be transferred to the paper by the crayon.
3. Place the paper against another texture and transfer this texture to another portion of the drawing.
4. Textures may be repeated or overlapped.
5. Unusual effects can be obtained by using several colors.

Supplies

1. Wax crayon
2. Thin drawing paper
3. Pencil
4. Textured surface

Crayon Shavings

Supplies

1. Old electric iron
2. Wax crayons
3. Paper
4. Knife
5. Cardboard

Procedure

1. Make a simple rack to hold the electric iron with the ironing surface up.
2. Shave the wax crayons with a knife, catching the shavings on a piece of paper fastened to cardboard. Push the shavings around until the image is created.
3. Pass the paper above the heated iron until the crayon shavings begin to melt. Continue this process with additional crayon until the desired pattern is created.
4. Watercolor, crayons or tempera paint can be used to add detail to complete the picture.

NOTE: Care should be taken in this problem while handling the iron and knife.

ALSO: Heat sources other than the iron may be used to melt the shavings. The drawing may be laid in direct sunlight, on a radiator, or over a light bulb. Care should be taken in that too much exposure will make the wax run.

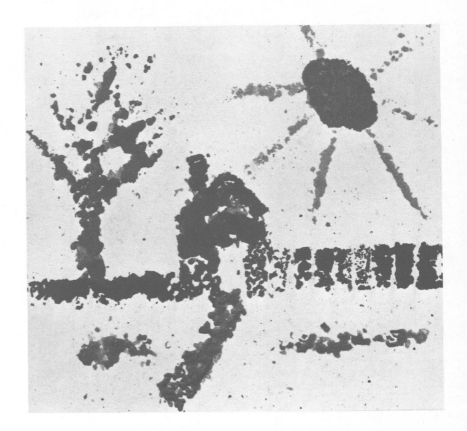

Crayon Textures

Procedure

1. Hold the drawing paper against a surface which has a definite texture and rub the crayon over the paper. The texture will be transferred to the paper by the crayon.
2. Place the paper against another texture and transfer this texture to the paper.
3. Textures may be repeated or overlapped.

Supplies

1. Wax crayon
2. Thin drawing paper
3. Pencil
4. Textured surface

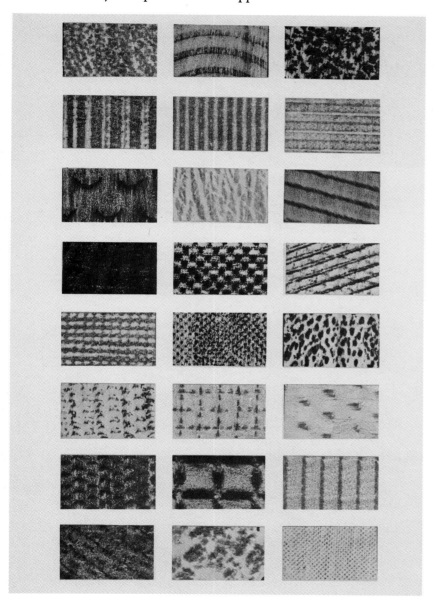

Crayon Transfer Print

Supplies

1. Paper
2. Colored chalk
3. Crayons
4. Pencil or ball-point pen

Procedure

1. Completely cover a sheet of white paper with a heavy coating of light-colored chalk.
2. Cover the coating of chalk with a very heavy layer of darker colored crayon.
3. Place a clean piece of white paper over the crayon and chalk-covered paper.
4. Using a dull pencil or ball-point pen, and using pressure, draw a design on the paper (Ill. 1).
5. The pressure causes the crayon to adhere to the underside of the top paper, which creates two separate designs (Ill. 2, 3).

Encaustic Painting

Encaustic is an old method of painting and pertains to the use of heated wax which contains colored pigment. However, encaustic painting is also possible without a hot plate by soaking fine crayon shavings in a small amount of turpentine for twelve to fifteen days. The finer the shaving, the quicker they dissolve. The dissolved crayons should be a smooth creamy medium for painting.

Procedure

1. Sort out the pieces of crayon in a muffin tin according to color.
2. To melt the crayons, heat the muffin tin with an electric hot plate or light bulb.
3. Paint directly on the chosen surface with the hot melted crayons. Many varied effects of luminosity, texture, and tone are unique to encaustic painting.

   NOTE: The addition of toluene (which should be obtainable through a chemistry department) in a volume equal to that of the melted crayon will facilitate the painting process by keeping the crayon in a liquid state. Toluene is extremely volatile and should be handled with caution.

Supplies

1. Wax crayons, or see formula for encaustic paint, page 246
2. Old muffin tin
3. A 100 or 150 watt light bulb and extension cord, or small electric hot plate (to be used in melting crayons)
4. Stiff bristle painting brushes (the use of melted crayon will render the brushes unusable for any other media)
5. Any durable painting surface (wood, canvas board, plaster, masonite, heavy cardboard, etc.)
6. Turpentine and soap for cleaning brush

Map Doodle

Supplies

1. Road map
2. Tracing paper (translucent)
3. Pencil
4. Crayons or paint

Procedure

1. Cover an area of the road map with a piece of tracing paper.
2. Look for shapes that are created by the roads on the map and draw them in with pencil. Many interesting abstract designs or subject matter can be found.
3. Crayon or paint the finished picture.

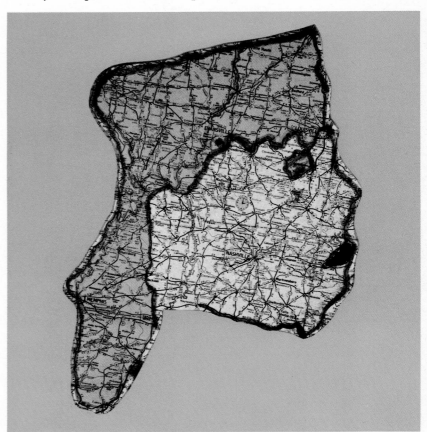

Melted Crayon

Procedure

1. Hold the crayon briefly over the flame of the candle until it softens, then press, drip, or drag the softened crayon onto the paper. A definite design or drawing can be sketched on the paper beforehand to serve as a guide, or the idea can be created with melted crayon directly.
2. Should the crayon become too short to hold over the flame, a long pin stuck into the crayon will solve this problem.
3. A number of different colors melted on top of one another will not only create an unusual textural effect, but will greatly enrich the color.

NOTE: As this problem involves the use of an open flame, it is suggested that every precaution be observed.

Supplies

1. Paper
2. Crayons with paper wrapping removed
3. Candle

Pressed Crayon Laminations

Supplies

1. Crayons
2. Wax paper
3. Iron
4. Knife or crayon sharpener
5. Newsprint or newspaper

Procedure

1. Shave the crayons on a piece of wax paper placed on newspaper, creating the image by pushing the shavings around with a small piece of cardboard.
2. Cover the crayon-covered wax paper with another piece of wax paper.
3. Cover both pieces of wax paper with a piece of newspaper and iron with a warm iron.

NOTE: Variations are possible by cutting the wax laminations into various shapes and putting them into a design pressed again between two new sheets of wax paper. A string pressed between the wax sheets makes it adaptable for use in a mobile.

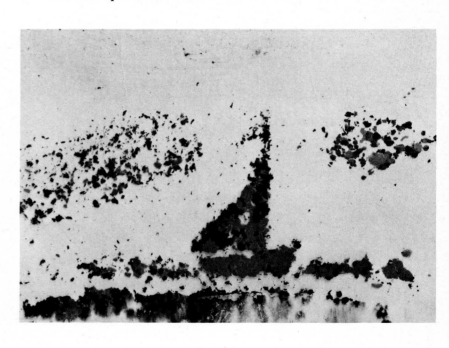

LETTERING

Principles of Lettering

Lettering and manuscript writing is an art which must conform to certain principles in order to be attractive and legible. There is no better time to learn these principles than in the formative years. There are, of course, many types of lettering and these are capable of many types of expression, i.e.,—speed, action, dignity, beauty, etc. However, the beginner should not venture too far from the simpler forms of lettering, and for this reason only the fundamental rules of the Gothic letter structure are illustrated here. A variety of lettering can be created from this basic type, as is indicated in the accompanying illustration.

A basic letter with numerous variations.

Lettering is one of those rare areas in the field of art where definite rules seem justified. To help produce better learning and manuscript writing in the grades, a few simple guides are listed below. Each of these guidelines is subject to variation in more complicated styles, such as italic (slanted) or script.

It is recommended that a rough layout of the letters be done in pencil before inking.

Full consideration should be given to forms of the letters, size, placement of words on page, and spacing between letters and words.

Ink or Felt Pen Lettering

Procedure

1. The axes of all Gothic letters are perpendicular to the line upon which they rest, and are of uniform thickness.

PERPENDICULAR | perpendicular

2. Capitals or upper case letters are all the same height—usually two spaces high for children.

A B C D E F G H I J K L M N
O P Q R S T U V W X Y Z ·
1 2 3 4 5 6 7 8 9 0

3. Capital letters are of three different width groups—wide, average, and narrow.

Narrow Letters   Wide Letters

E F I J L T   G M O Q W

There are no serifs or dots on the basic Gothic letters I or J, as indicated above, unless used on all letters.

4. A serif is a cross stroke on the end of the individual lines of a letter.

COLOR ART CRAFT

5. Horizontal line intersections generally should be above or below the middle of the letter for greater legibility.

Letters with horizontal line intersections above the middle:

B E F H X

Letters with horizontal line intersections below the middle:

A G K P R Y

6. Correct spacing is absolutely necessary to make lettering or manuscript writing legible and attractive. Measured spacing produces a lack of unity in lettered words. Spacing should be done with feeling for the *area between* the letters. Leave the width of an average letter between words when lettering.

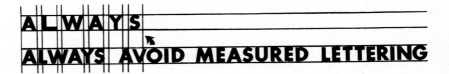

7. Lower case, or small letters, are usually divided into thirds for the convenience of young children.

abcdefghijklmnop
qrstuvwxyz

8. The lower case Gothic alphabet can be divided into three families of letters:

Short letters

aceimnorsuvwxz

Letters with ascenders

bdfhklt

(note that the letter t extends only halfway into the top space)

Letters with descenders

gjpqy

Cut Paper Letters

Procedure

1. As all capital letters are of the same height, cut a strip of paper to the dimensions of the proposed lettering.

2. Although all capitals are of the same height, the widths vary in being either narrow, average, or wide. Cut the strip into pieces representing the width of average letters, narrow letters, and wide letters. When cutting the letters from the piece make sure that the thicknesses within each type (average, narrow, wide) are all uniform.

average   narrow   wide

3. The following diagrams differentiate between the average, narrow, and wide letters and show how some can be folded and cut. Experience will eliminate the need of sketching each letter with pencil before cutting.

    When the fold occurs in the middle of the letter (as in A, H, V, Y, M, X, W, E, F, and T) the letter must be cut half of its intended width at that point, as this width will double when the paper is opened out.

Supplies

1. Lightweight paper (typing paper works well)
2. Scissors
3. Pencil
4. Ruler
5. Paste or rubber cement

Average Width Letters:
A B D H K N P R S U V X Y Z

Fold in half and cut around the corner to form the curved edge of the letter.

Fold top edge to middle crease, and cut opening as illustrated.

Fold bottom edge up to the bottom of the top opening and cut larger opening, as illustrated.

Unfold and cut out triangle. The bottom of the letter B will be larger than the top.

This letter K is cut without folding the paper.

The N cannot be folded to cut.

Fold top edge down below the middle and cut out shape as illustrated.

The opening in the letter R is cut like the P; the remainder of the letter is cut without folding.

Cut away the excess paper from the figure 8 to form the letter S.

The Z cannot be folded to cut.

Narrow Letters: E F I J L T

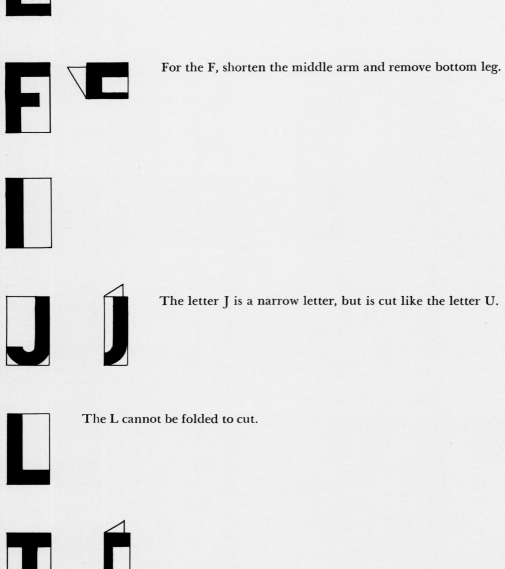

Shorten the middle arm of the E.

For the F, shorten the middle arm and remove bottom leg.

The letter J is a narrow letter, but is cut like the letter U.

The L cannot be folded to cut.

Wide Letters: C G M O Q W

Fold paper in half, then in half again. Cut quarter circle for both outside and inside of letter.

Open and cut away the section indicated.

Open and cut away the parts indicated.

The sides of the M are vertical.

Fold paper in half, then in half again. Cut quarter circle for both outside and inside of letter.

Open and cut away the extra tail.

The sides of the W slant.

4. The top or bottom of the following letters can either be pointed or flat, but all must be of the same style when used together in forming a word. Poined letters should extend either above or below the line.

AA VV NN ZZ
WW MM

5. Simple three-dimensional lettering is interesting to use and easy to make.

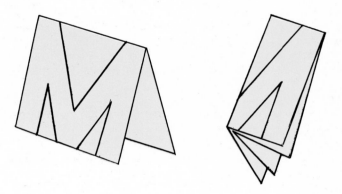

Fold a sheet of paper so that it is twice the height of the intended letter. Fold the paper in half again if the letter can be folded to cut. Make sure when cutting that each letter is held together by some part of the fold.

Mount the bottom of the letters on a poster or bulletin board—the spring in the paper will give the top half a three-dimensional effect.

Paper Strip Letters

Procedure

1. Cut paper strips of uniform width.
2. Form the letters as illustrated, adjusting the paper to the desired size. Cut off the excess portion of the strip, if any.
3. Glue the parts of the letters as necessary.
4. Apply glue to the bottom edge of each letter in turn, and fix in place to form desired words.

Supplies

1. Paper
2. Scissors
3. Paste or glue

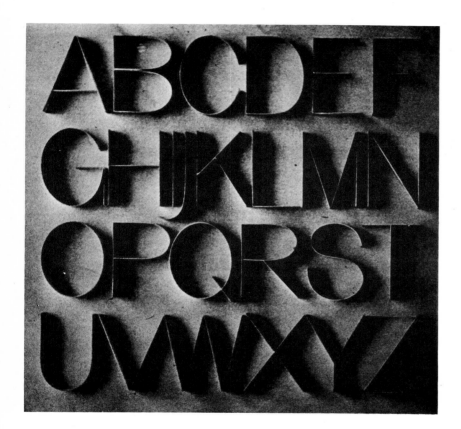

MATTING AND FRAMING

Mat Proportions

The matting of display material is an additional cost, but it makes displays more effective, and is a practical method of retaining and storing outstanding material. It should be pointed out that display material of similar size is interchangeable, enabling the mat to be used more than once.

For effective and proper matting of creative art work and other display material, the following rules generally apply:

The optical center of a picture area is always a certain distance above the measured center. Measured centering of a work in a mat therefore creates a top-heavy appearance, whereas optical centering creates greater frontality and balance, and more comfortable viewing.

1. In matting a square illustration the top and sides of the mat should be equal, with the bottom margin wider.
2. In matting a horizontal rectangular illustration the bottom margin is the widest, and the top margin should be smaller than the sides.
3. In matting a vertical rectangular illustration the bottom margin is the widest, and the top margin wider than the sides.

Cutting a Mat

Supplies

1. Mat board (pebbled or smooth, colored or white)
2. Cardboard (which should be of the same rigidity as the mat board)
3. Pencil
4. Ruler
5. Mat knife, or single-edge razor blade
6. Gummed tape

Procedure

1. Cut the mat board large enough to accommodate the picture to be matted, including a generous margin (Ill. 1).
2. Cut a piece of cardboard of equal dimensions. This piece will be the backing for the finished mat (Ill. 2).
3. Using the suggestions for square, horizontal, or vertical pictures mentioned earlier, measure and draw a light line the size of the opening to be cut on the face of the mat board (Ill. 3). Be sure that these lines are drawn at least one-half of an inch smaller than both the length and width of the actual picture to be mounted. This will allow the mat to overlap the picture on all sides.
4. Place a piece of heavy scrap cardboard under the line to be cut. Cut carefully along the pencil lines with a sharp mat knife, or single-edge razor blade. Apply enough pressure on the tool to cut through the mat with one cut. A ruler held firmly will serve as a guide while cutting. If the cutting tool is held at a 45-degree angle a beveled edge can be cut—but only after considerable practice (Ill. 4).

5. Turn the mat over and butt the top edge of the second piece of cardboard. Hinge the two pieces together with gummed tape (Ill. 5).

6. Close the mat on the cardboard with the window opening facing up. Mark the four corners of the opening on the cardboard backing with a sharp pencil. This will help in locating the picture directly behind the window (Ill. 6).

7. Open the mat again and center the picture behind the window, making sure that the closed mat overlaps the picture on all four sides (Ill. 7).

8. Fasten the picture to the cardboard along the top edge with gummed tape (Ill. 8), making sure that the tape does not overlap the work far enough to be seen when the mat is closed. A picture fastened this way is easily removed and replaced with another without harm to the mat.

9. Finished matted picture (Ill. 9).

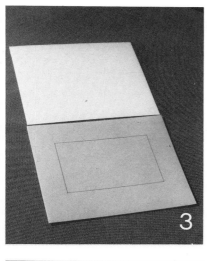
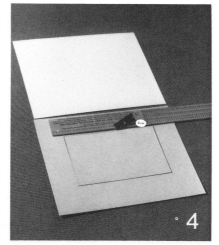
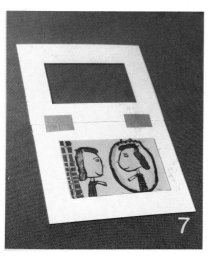
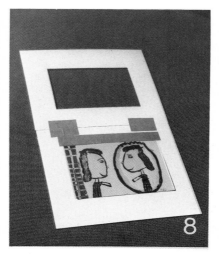
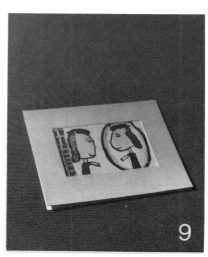

Mounted Picture Mat

Supplies

1. Picture to be matted
2. Mat board or colored cardboard
3. Rubber cement
4. Scissors, sharp knife or single-edge razor blade
5. Pencil
6. Ruler

Procedure

1. Choose picture to be mounted and cut it to the desired size.
2. Cut material to be used as mat large enough to accommodate the picture to be mounted, including a generous margin. Use matting proportions for square, horizontal, or vertical pictures on pages 112 and 113 as a guide.
3. Place the cut picture on the mounting material, and use a ruler to make sure the border proportions are correct.
4. Draw around the picture with a light pencil line.
5. Remove the picture and apply rubber cement to the pencil-enclosed area. Allow to dry.
6. Apply rubber cement to the back of the picture and allow it to dry.
7. Carefully replace the picture in the penciled shape. Lay a clean piece of paper over the illustration and smooth it with the hand.

Shadowbox Frame

Procedure

1. Mount the picture or print to be framed on a piece of cardboard the size of the interior of the box. The edges of the colored cardboard may be left exposed around the picture (Ill. 1).
2. Cut four cardboard strips with a 45° angle at each end (Ill. 2). The shortest dimension of each strip should be slightly shorter than the box.
3. Glue these four strips at the corners to form a flat frame (Ill. 2).
4. Glue decorative trim to flat frame (Ill. 3).
5. Glue mounted picture in the bottom of the box (Ill. 4).
6. Glue the decorative flat frame to the top edge of the box (Ill. 5).
7. Glue picture hanger or cardboard support to the back of the box (Ill. 6).

Supplies

1. Picture to be framed
2. Shallow cardboard box, slightly larger than picture
3. Colored cardboard for mounting picture
4. Colored framing strips
5. Glue
6. Rubber cement for mounting picture
7. Trim for frame
8. Scissors or knife

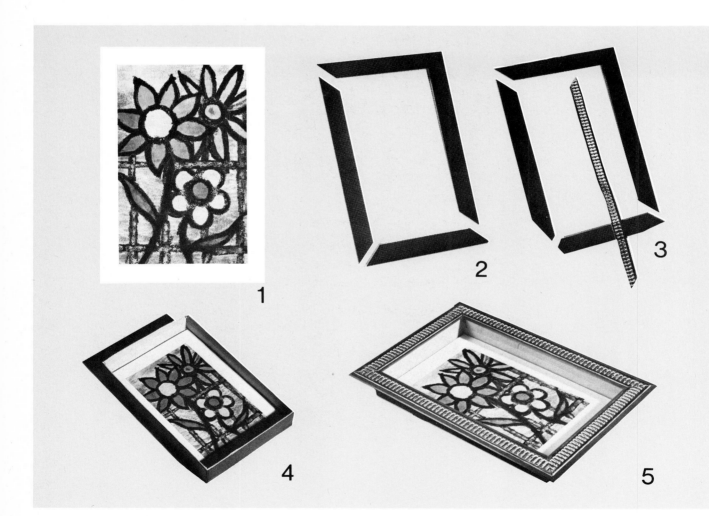

6

Three-Dimensional Picture Frame

Procedure

1. Choose the picture to be framed and mount with rubber cement on a piece of cardboard, allowing at least 1½ inches of cardboard on all sides (Ill. 1).
2. Score around the edge of the mounted picture deep enough so it can be bent forward.
3. Cut out four V-shaped corners. The larger the V, the deeper the frame (Ill. 2).
4. Turn up all sides until corners meet.
5. Hold corners together and tape on back.
6. To hang, place a piece of tape across two ends of a loop of string, fastening them toward the top of the back.

Supplies

1. Cardboard or mat board
2. Ruler
3. Scissors, single-edge razor blade, or knife
4. Pencil
5. Rubber cement

1

2

MURALS

Murals

A mural is a large work of art usually designed for a specific location and intended to be viewed by large numbers of people.

A small mural may be produced by the individual student, and a larger work is readily adaptable to classroom work as a group enterprise. As such, and because of its mass audience, it can be developed from a theme of general interest selected from any subject area. Properly handled it can be an effective educational aid.

The quality of art work in a class-produced mural can be easily diluted by its commitment to subject and audience. (A review of the section on "Basic Concepts of Art Instruction" will refresh the reader on the perils inherent in the subjugaton of art to other disciplines.) From an art standpoint little is to be gained from the mural if it is to be confined to a strictly factual presentation. On the other hand, much may be gained if the subject under consideration is studied and researched (on a collective and personal basis) and then submitted to the interpretive abilities of the students. Under such a system of instruction the students could freely debate and vote on the general presentation of the theme, and volunteer for selected passages of this theme. The overall plan or layout of the composition could be left in the hands of one student or it could be produced by the instructor, *providing* the sketch is not too specific or rigid.

As a public work of art some consideration should be given to effective place of the mural in terms of traffic, lighting, and other factors. When the location has been determined the space available will help to decide the total shape of the mural. Architecture may be a friend or foe, but in any case must be considered.

Students participating in the design of a mural should be of a narrow age range. When older students are mixed with younger children there is often an unfortunate tendency to compare. Actually, when ages vary, the products are non-comparable, but this is not always understood, and the general reaction could be frustrating and embarrassing to some students.

When the main composition has been sketched, the surface (wrapping paper is cheap, strong, and quite adequate) may be divided up into a working area for each student. Because of spatial restrictions it is not always possible to have all artists working simultaneously. Work could proceed on a shift basis, integrating this project with other scheduled activities.

It is usually advisable to restrict the work on a mural to one or two media. Materials are variable in strength, and the design could be chaotic if all media were used, unless they were subject to some type of coordination. Some media, such as chalk, are perfectly satisfactory but quite impermanent, and could be easily smudged during the progress of the work. In avoiding this a fixative or plastic spray could be used to protect the drawing, but this would ruin the surface for further drawing. Crayon is cheap and permanent, and poster paint is effective, but may flake off if the mural is rolled up or mistreated. Cut paper is a simple and effective medium, and is easily combined with other media. Collage techniques may be employed by pasting up fabrics and other textured materials, and papier collé may be used according to the instructions under the problem "Magazine Collé."

The narrative by Jean Hasselschwert which follows is a fascinating first-person account of her direction of the painting of a mural. The remarkable thing about the project is that it was designed and executed by *all* of the students in kindergarten, first, second and third grades of the school, each of them having a section to paint. In addition, the mural is not only heroic in scale, but also a permanent decorative feature of the building. This is an excellent example of cooperation between an enterprising teacher, an enlightened school administration, and some very enthusiastic children:

Inspired by a slide-lecture, several teachers approached me about coordinating a special art project to beautify and, perhaps engender new pride in Kenwood Elementary School. They felt I might be interested in such an undertaking because of my background in public school art and the fact that our children attend Kenwood School.

After a meeting of the teachers and the principal, we decided to paint a mural on the upper portion of one wall of the primary wing, extending 200 feet, and measuring approximately 4 feet in height. The project would be supplementary in nature, with the children of the kindergarten through third grades playing the major role in this project and the teachers assuming an advisory position. We quickly and easily enlisted the financial aid of the P.T.A. and the Student Council.

Murals, past and present, were discussed at an assembly of all participants. What is a mural? Does it have a theme? How do the artists use color? How do the artists tie all the parts of the mural together?

Finally, we considered the possibility of the children painting a mural of their own directly on the hallway wall. The excitement generated by this thought was fantastic and the questions came quickly. Who would paint? Everyone would have an equal part in planning and painting the mural. What would be the theme? The theme which would tie the mural together would be the question, "What is the most interesting, exciting, or unique thing about Kenwood School?"

Each class began planning their own section, beginning with discussions and idea sketches in crayon. We found this phase of the project to be the most difficult, but possibly the most valuable as a review of previous lessons in all areas, including art. Special interest groups were formed and individual problems were handled on an individual basis. The scale of the drawings was a particular problem, and to solve it, the children enlarged their drawings on large pieces of wrapping paper (Ill. 1, 2, 3) and cut them out like big paper dolls.

During this period, the sixth grades assisted us in the project by painting "block-out" white over the cement blocks (Ill. 4) which would be the ground for our painting. The space below the mural was covered with brown wrapping paper and the children began arranging their cut-out shapes on the paper (Ill. 5). Small loops of masking tape were placed on the back of the cut-outs so that they could be moved and easily rearranged. For the first time, we could see all the class sections joined together.

After a short talk concerning the "art of climbing," we were ready to move the cut-outs up on the wall directly above their position on the brown paper. The children traced around the cutouts with large drawing pencils (Ill. 6, 7), added the details and returned the paper cutouts to their places on the wrapping paper, where they could be used for future reference.

A semi-gloss latex paint, available in brilliant colors, was selected. The bright semi-gloss colors would lighten the dark hallway and the

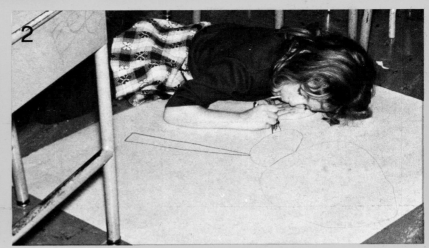

latex paint would simplify the handling and clean-up chores. Brushes of various sizes were purchased, along with rollers and sponges. Empty oleo containers with snap lids were collected to hold and store small quantities of paint. Old shirts to be used as smocks were collected and we were ready to paint.

Four children were allowed on each scaffold at one time, and we had three scaffolds in use. Other children assisted by handing paint to the artists, washing brushes and wiping up any spills. The painting shifts were changed every thirty to forty-five minutes so that each child would have a number of chances to paint. The atmosphere was very relaxed after the children were assured that any drips could be removed or covered and shaky outlines could be straightened after the latex dried.

The children began by painting the figures and objects (Ill. 8). The background was organized later, and large areas of color were used to tie the sections of each class together. Spectrum values were used, saving black and white for outlining and details. Brilliantly colored trees, animals and figures soon began to take shape on our wall.

After a lesson on sponge printing, the children began to add pattern to the mural (Ill. 9). They cut out sponge shapes to print flowers on dresses, spots on animals, stripes on shirts and features on faces.

The week before summer vacation, the brown paper, with its bedraggled cut-out shapes, was removed and our mural was finished. The painting has retained all the charm and spontaneity found in children's art (Ill. 10). After five months of art, the children had completed a beautiful, meaningful work of art. Special thanks must go to the principal and teachers who gave their ideas and time, always with enthusiasm and good humor, to make the mural a reality. They are:

Mrs. Cheryl Huther, Kindergarten
Miss Sue Fehlner, First Grade
Mrs. Ruth Eisenhour, First Grade
Mrs. Virginia Draney, Second Grade
Mrs. Georgia Cross, Second Grade
Mrs. Eva Row, Third Grade
Mrs. Diane Ashbaugh, Third Grade
Mr. Harland Lehtomaa, Principal

PAINT AND INK

Nature of the Medium

Watercolor

Watercolor is a brilliant, transparent, water-soluble painting medium. The pigment is available as color blocks in pans, or in the more expensive and professional tubes.

The distinguishing property of watercolor is the sparkling quality resulting from its transparency. Most painters strive for a spontaneous effect by utilizing the whiteness of the paper and the fluid blending of the colors. Watercolor requires planning, as does any art form, but there can be a good deal of improvisation. Unlike oil paintings, watercolors are worked up quickly, and rarely reworked.

The prerequisite to the successful use of watercolor is familiarity with its effects, achieved only through experimentation. Prior to painting the paper should be dampened; after this one should try bold, wet washes, with intermingled colors. Bold and fine strokes should be attempted, both wet and dry. One can also try wet-on-dry techniques, blotting, tilting the paper to control the flow of color, various resists, and combinations of watercolor with other media. For serious efforts, it is recommended that the paper be fastened to a board with paper tape after soaking, to allow the painting to dry without distortion of the paper.

Three types of paper are available for watercolor painting:

Hot-pressed: a smooth paper, for detailed work
Cold-pressed: moderate texture, and the most common
Rough: highly-textured surface, producing clear, sharp effects

These are the more "professional" papers beyond the needs and means of most children. A paper of fairly heavy weight should be used, however; manila (or its equivalent) is a satisfactory, inexpensive paper for general classroom use.

Brushes used for watercolor painting should be washed frequently, and the cleaning water should be replaced often. Smocks or aprons are useful, as are newspapers and paper towels. Expect a mess; it's the only way to learn!

Tempera Paint

Tempera is a water-soluble paint which is available as liquid or dry powder. It is an extremely versatile medium for classroom experiences in art, and works well on a variety of surfaces. (When painted on non-porous materials, a small amount of liquid detergent should be added.)

Tempera may be spread by brush, roller, sponge, stick, or, if slightly reduced with water, it can be sprayed. Lights and darks are controlled by additions of white or black.

Unlike watercolor, tempera is an opaque medium; the appearance of the paper is not such a factor, nor does it have to be stretched. The paint may be mixed semi-dry, and built up to create a textured surface. The others possibilities are too great to list here, but include the following: screen printing, block-printing, finger painting and lettering.

Young children using a potentially messy medium such as tempera should wear smocks, if possible. Clear water should be kept handy for keeping brushes clean. Small plastic or paper cups can be provided for the various colors.

Inks

A liquid vehicle and a soluble pigment are required for making ink, and this is satisfactory only if it can flow evenly, and has good tinting strength. The earliest ink known, black carbon, was prepared by the early Egyptians and Chinese. This was followed by iron-gall (from growths on trees), bistre (burnt wood), and sepia, a secretion from cuttle fish). Today there is a wide variety of inks, transparent and opaque, water-soluble and waterproof. Perhaps the type best known to the art student is India ink, which is really a waterproof carbon black. All of these inks serve effectively for *line* drawings; drawing *washes* are usually produced with ink sticks or water colors. A tremendous number of inks can be made with fruit and vegetable juices, aniline and coal dyes.

Pen and ink drawings are generally characterized by their clarity and precision. This, of course, can be modified by choice of instrument or method of control. It takes a great many strokes to produce an area of tone, and this is the principal reason why pen and ink drawings are best created on a fairly small scale.

Pens

Those of us who take our familiar metal pen points of various kinds for granted may not realize that they are fairly new, not having been successfully developed until the last century. Until that time, the reed pen had been the pen of the ancients, and the quill pen the principal instrument from the medieval period to modern times. Most of us probably remember the use of quill pens in the drawings of Rembrandt, and in the historical documents drawn up by the founders of our Republic.

Today, the advent of ball, felt and plastic tip pens have revolutionized the writing industry, as well as providing artisis with yet another drawing tool. Artists, however, still make use of the earlier pen types on occasion, and even resort, at times, to match sticks and other unlikely things for making ink marks on paper. Each drawing instrument leaves its own distinctive mark and, for the artist, has its own special interests and disciplines. In the hands of children, the mechanical metal points and felt and plastic tips are generally more suitable, but other kinds of pens might provide some exciting moments for the older child.

Blottos

Supplies

1. Paper
2. Watercolor, or thin tempera paint
3. Scissors
4. Paste

Procedure

1. Cut a number of paper squares and rectangles of various sizes.
2. Crease each paper square in the middle so that later it can be folded easily.
3. Sprinkle a few drops of paint on one side of the crease.
4. Fold the paper on the creased line with the paint inside and press—this causes the paint to be squeezed into various and interesting shapes.
5. When the paper is opened the result will be surprising—it might resemble an insect, flower, butterfly, or any number of items.
6. After a number of blottos are made, cut them out and arrange them into a picture or pattern. When satisfied with the arrangement, paste them in place on a piece of paper of desired size.

NOTE: After experimenting it will be possible to control the results by placing the paint according to a predetermined pattern.

Don't overlook the possibility of using several colors in one blotto or the adding of details with other media.

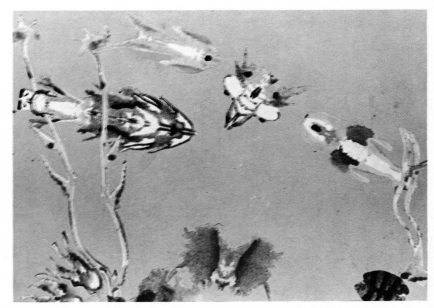

Drawing with Ink

Procedure

1. Pen and ink drawing is capable of great interest if approached in an experimental manner. For instance, pen points of different types create varied lines and these lines in turn may be combined with each other to create stippled, cross-hatched, scumbled, and other textural effects.

2. Brush and ink drawing is a highly expressive medium due to the flexibility of the brush line. The quality of line may be controlled by the type of brush (bristle or sable), wide or narrow, fully or sparsely haired; the hand pressure applied; the quantity of ink carried by the brush; and the calculating or spontaneous attitude of the artist.

   As in most drawing, greater freedom is obtained from the brush by avoiding the grip used in writing. Instead one may hold the brush between the thumb and forefingers while supporting the hand on the other three fingers. The movement of the brush should be initiated with the body ("body english") and directed through the arm. Drawing done with the fingers or wrists is more suited to the development of surface details.

3. Stick and ink is a lesser known drawing procedure, but one which has enough individuality to justify its frequent use. In technique it is very simple—one merely dips an absorbent piece of wood into the ink, allows it to become semi-saturated and draws as one would with a pen. Interesting effects may be obtained by using sticks with frayed, sharp, broad, and smooth ends.

NOTE: Ink is very effective when used with other media. It may be added to watercolor, tempera, and crayon to enhance the brilliance of colors or provide accents and outline. The above may, in turn, be used over ink. When ink is used on wet paper, the results are unexpected and interesting.

Supplies

1. Pen
2. Brush
3. Soft wood sticks of various types (match sticks, sucker sticks, etc.)
4. Ink
5. Paper

Felt Tip Pen Drawing

Supplies

1. Paper, paper-covered object, or cloth
2. Multicolored felt tip pens
3. Pencil
4. Clear spray

Procedure

1. Until confidence is gained, use preliminary light outline drawing in pencil on paper.
2. Areas of the drawing can now be filled in with colored felt tip pens.
3. To prevent possible smudging, spray with clear spray.

NOTE: Part of the fun of drawing with felt tip pens is experimenting for new effects.

Finger Painting

Procedure

1. Soak the paper in water in any of the following ways, making sure both sides are thoroughly wet.

   a. Put the paper under the faucet in a sink, or
   b. Roll the paper into a tube and submerge it in a container of water, or
   c. Spread the paper on a table and soak it with sponge and water. The paper adheres more firmly to a surface if wet on both sides.

2. Place the wet paper on a smooth and flat surface. Do not place it too close to the edge of the table top, as the paint may drip over. Make sure the glossy side of the paper is up and all wrinkles and air bubbles are smoothed out. Satisfactory finger paintings cannot be made on an uneven or unsteady surface.

3. Place approximately one tablespoonful of finger paint on the wet paper—if powdered finger paint is used, sift it lightly over the entire paper—more can be applied later if necessary. Paint applied too heavily will crack or chip off when dry.

4. Spread the paint evenly over the entire surface of paper with the palm of the hand or forearm to create the background of the finger painting.

5. Varied movements of the hands and forearms in various positions will create interesting effects. The side of the hand when held rigid and pulled over paper makes long and delicate leaves. This same hand position moved in a zig-zag motion creates an altogether different effect. Experiment with a variety of hand and arm movements and positions. An infinte number of effects are possible by using the closed fist, bent fingers, open palm, heel of the hand, wrist, etc. Other various effects can also be obtained by using a comb, a small notched piece of cardboard, etc. Areas of color can also be cleaned away with a sponge.

6. New beginnings can be made until the paper loses its gloss. Sprinkle a few drops of water on the paper if the finger paint becomes too sticky to allow the hand or arm to slide easily over the paper.

7. Spread the paper or newspaper on the floor in a seldom used area. Lift the finger painting by two corners and lay it on some newspapers.

8. Allow the painting to dry. Press it on the unpainted side with a hot iron.

NOTE: It is suggested that only a few children work at one time unless a large room with adequate table space is available. Finger paintings can be used to decorate items of many kinds, including knitting boxes, wastebaskets, book jackets, portfolio covers, etc.

Colored paper cut to particular shapes and pasted in place on finger paintings adds further detail.

A stencil cut from paper and pasted over a finger painting is another variation.

If finger painting is used as a decorative covering it should be sprayed with clear plastic spray or painted with shellac for permanence.

Supplies

1. Finger paint (recipe on page 246)
2. Glossy or glazed paper
3. Sponge
4. Iron
5. Plastic spray or white shellac
6. Water must be available in a sink or large container, to soak the paper

Finger Painting over Crayon

Procedure

1. Cover the paper with brightly colored crayon.
2. Lay the crayoned paper on a smooth flat surface.
3. Spread liquid starch over the crayon.
4. Sprinkle a small amount of tempera paint in liquid starch. Be sure that its color contrasts with the crayon color(s).
5. The color will mix as soon as the hand is drawn over the surface.

NOTE: See page 133 for finger painting instructions.

Supplies

1. Drawing paper
2. Liquid starch
3. Powdered tempera
4. Crayons

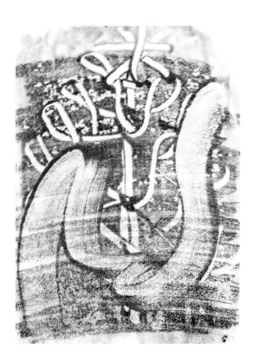

Ink or Felt Pen on Cloth

Supplies

1. Colored waterproof drawing ink
2. Cloth—unbleached muslin, silk, rayon, etc.
3. Brush, lettering pen, or felt pen
4. White blotting paper
5. Smooth flat board

Procedure

1. Make a drawing or design with the pencil directly on the blotting paper.
2. Place the fabric directly over the drawing.
3. Painting with ink can begin when the drawing can be seen through the cloth due to its transparency. The blotter on which the pencil drawing was made creates an absorbent surface which will take up any excess paint.

NOTE: Do not use too much ink on the brush, but paint in a "dry brush" technique. Large areas should be built up with textures, such as dots, cross-hatching, series of dashes, etc.

Soda Straw Painting

Procedure

1. Place several little pools of variously colored paint on the paper with a brush.
2. Point the end of the straw at the pools of paint and blow in the direction the paint is meant to move.
3. Overlapping of colors creates numerous effects in blending colors.
4. Add details when dry.

Supplies

1. Paper
2. Watercolor paint, or thin tempera
3. Soda straws
4. Brush

Sponge Painting

Supplies

1. Sponge
2. Scissors
1. Dry or liquid tempera paint
4. Paper

Procedure

1. Soak the paper thoroughly in water.
2. Lay the wet paper on a smooth surface and remove all the wrinkles and excess water.
3. Use pieces of moist sponge which have been cut into small shapes and use as a brush by dipping them into the tempera paint.

Tempera Painting on Damp Paper

Procedure

1. Soak the paper thoroughly in water.
2. Lay the wet paper on a desk top or drawing board and smooth out all the wrinkles.
3. Blot up any pools of water with blotting material.
4. Paint directly on the damp paper. Make sure to use more pigment than water, for the colors tend to lose their brilliance when dry. Paint light colors first, and second and third colors before the paper dries, so colors will mingle and blend into spontaneous and soft shapes. After the paint is applied, avoid reworking.
5. Leave some areas unpainted to add sparkle.
6. Details, if necessary, can be painted in when the painting is dry.

NOTE: Damp paper tempera painting must be done hurriedly to be lively. Don't expect complete success on the first try, for only experience will tell just how wet the paper must be and how much paint should be used. Clean the brush and the water in the container often.

Supplies

1. Dry or liquid tempera paint
2. Brush
3. Paper
4. Water container
5. Blotting material (rag, sponge, paper towel, etc.)

Tempera Resist

Supplies

1. Tempera paints
2. Brush
3. Paper
4. Higgins India ink

Procedure

1. Paint some areas of the paper with tempera as necessary to suggest the design. By all means leave much of the paper unpainted, thus making provision for the absorption of the ink by these areas. The paint used should be fairly heavy body.
2. When the paint is completely dry, paint over everything, tempera and paper, with India ink.
3. When the ink is dry, hold the drawing under running water, allowing the force of the water to dislodge the ink. Should this ink prove stubborn, its removal may be speeded by light strokes of the finger. A certain amount of caution should be exercised in removing the ink. Excessive washing could remove too much of the paint and ink. However, many seeming disasters have turned out beautifully at second glance. Furthermore, any lost color can be replaced with watercolor, ink, crayon, or tempera.

Watercolor and Rubber Cement Resist

Procedure

1. Paint a picture on the paper with rubber cement. Use the brush attached to the rubber cement jar or apply with a finger.
2. Allow the rubber cement to dry.
3. Paint over the rubber cement picture with watercolor paint. Several colors can be mingled together. The rubber cement will resist the paint.
4. Allow the paint to dry.
5. Clean away the rubber cement with an eraser and expose the paper and original drawing.

NOTE: Rubber cement can be painted over the areas previously painted with watercolor and repeated as often as desired. Make sure each is dry before applying the other.

Supplies

1. Watercolor paint
2. Paper
3. Rubber cement
4. Brush
5. Eraser

Watercolor Painting on Damp Paper

Supplies

1. Transparent watercolors
2. Brush
3. Drawing paper
4. Water container
5. Blotting material (rag, sponge, paper towels, etc.)

Procedure

1. Soak the paper thoroughly in water.
2. Lay the wet paper on a desk top or drawing board and smooth out all wrinkles.
3. Blot up any pools of water with the blotting material.
4. Paint directly on this damp paper. Make sure to use more pigment than water, for colors tend to lose their brilliance when dry. Paint the light colors first, and add second and third colors before paper dries, so colors will mingle and blend into spontaneous and soft shapes. After paint is applied, avoid reworking.
5. Leave some areas unpainted to add sparkle.
6. Details, if necessary, can be painted in when the painting is dry.

NOTE: Damp paper watercolors must be painted hurriedly to be lively. Don't expect complete success on the first try, for only experience will tell just how wet the paper must be and how much paint to use. Clean the brush and the water in the container often.

Watercolor Wax Resist

Procedure

1. Place wax paper over the drawing paper.
2. Draw heavily on the wax paper with pencil or the wooden end of a brush. The pressure will transfer the wax to the drawing paper.
3. Remove the wax paper and paint over the drawing with transparent watercolor. The lines drawn with the pencil will remain white.

NOTE: Drawing with paraffin or a wax candle will achieve the same result as the wax paper.

Supplies

1. Wax paper
2. Paper
3. Pencil
4. Transparent watercolors
5. Brush
6. Water container

PAPER AND CARDBOARD

Cardboard Relief

Supplies

1. Soft cardboard (tablet backing, shirt boards, etc.)
2. Glue
3. Scissors
4. Paint
5. Brush

Procedure

1. Cut a cardboard base on which to build a design.
2. Cut a second piece of cardboard into shapes of different sizes and glue to the cardboard base.
3. Cut a third piece of cardboard into shapes smaller in size than the previous pieces and glue in place.
4. Continue to cut and glue smaller pieces until a design of different levels results.
5. Cut and add details if necessary.

Colored Tissue Paper

Procedure

1. Fold and cut (or sketch, then cut) simple, bold shapes from colored tissue.
2. Arrange these shapes on a white mounting board, overlapping to achieve the most pleasing design and color effects.
3. Cover the tissue paper shapes with rubber cement and gently adhere them to the mounting board.

   NOTE: Boxes, jars, bottles and trays may be sprayed with white enamel and then decorated in the above manner. Articles to be decorated must be clean and sprayed according to the directions on the can of enamel. Apply tissue shapes which have been coated with rubber cement to the article, spreading smooth so that there are no wrinkles. Remove excess rubber cement with a ball of dried rubber cement, using care, as the tissue tears easily. If desired, additional decorative effects may be added with gold paint and brush to highlight tissue designs. When the paint is dry, spray the entire article with clear enamel to protect designs. Several thin coats, allowed to dry between applications, are necessary.

Supplies

1. Colored tissue in many colors
2. Rubber cement
3. Sharp scissors
4. White mounting board
5. Small brush

Colored Tissue Transparent Discs

Supplies

1. Tissue paper in many bright colors
2. Fine and medium basket reed
3. Masking tape
4. Rubber cement or white glue
5. Sharp scissors

Procedure

1. Soak the larger reed in water until it can be bent into circles without breaking. (A fine reed may bend without being soaked.)
2. Cut to make the size circle desired, using the fine reed for the small circles and the medium reed for the larger ones.
3. Overlap the ends of the reed at least one-half inch on the small circles and more on the larger ones, then fasten with small strips of masking tape. Allow the reed to dry thoroughly. (It may be easier to allow the reed to dry partially before fastening with masking tape, as the tape will hold better.)
4. Cut a circle out of tissue paper a little larger than the reed frame.
5. Apply white glue or rubber cement to the reed and press onto the tissue circle.
6. Cut tissue designs in various colors.
7. Cover the design with rubber cement and place on tissue circle. Two, three or more tissue designs may be placed one on top of another to achieve a really beautiful effect. These may be of the same color or different colors. Only by experimenting can the possibilities be realized.
8. Trim away the tissue extending beyond the frame.

NOTE: Above all, for the best results, work neatly. Draw the circles with a compass and handle the tissue gently when applying rubber cement. The decorative discs may be used as units in a mobile, to decorate windows, plastic bottles, glass panels, or put on straight reed stems and arranged in a container as a bouquet. They will resemble decorated lollipops!

Corrugated Cardboard

Method A

Procedure

1. Cut out pieces of colored construction paper, or corrugated cardboard, or both.
2. Paste these pieces on a piece of corrugated cardboard to form the desired pattern.
3. Accents can be added with ink, tempera paint, or crayon.

Supplies

1. Corrugated cardboard
2. Scissors
3. Colored paper
4. Paste or rubber cement
5. Ink, paint, or crayon

Method B

Procedure

1. Cut through the paper surface of a corrugated cardboard box with a *sharp knife* and peel out areas to expose the corrugations.
2. Color can be added with paints or crayons when the picture is complete.

Supplies

1. Corrugated cardboard box
2. Sharp knife
3. Paint, ink, or crayons

Method C

Procedure

1. Interesting effects are created by painting directly on the corrugated cardboard. Try painting in the ridges, on top of the ridges, or across the ridges. Further interest may be obtained by using one color inside the ridges and another one on top of the ridges.

Supplies

1. Corrugated cardboard
2. Tempera paint
3. Brush
4. Water container

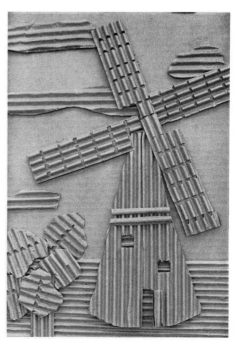

Cut Paper Design

Procedure

1. Fold the paper into as small a division as possible.
2. Cut numerous small shapes out of the paper until there is more paper cut away than there is remaining (Ill. 1).
3. Carefully unfold the paper so as not to tear it when opening.
4. The design can be mounted on a contrasting colored paper. Numerous designs can be created through an inventive approach using variously colored, shaped pieces under the cut design (Ill. 2).

Supplies

1. Thin paper
2. Scissors
3. Rubber cement

Distance Silhouette

Supplies

1. Colored paper
2. Scissors
3. Translucent paper (tracing paper, onion skin paper, tissue paper, etc.)
4. Rubber cement

Procedure

1. Make an outline drawing on paper with pencil.
2. Cut out the shapes to appear in the background and rubber cement them to a sheet of white paper (Ill. 1).
3. Place a piece of the translucent paper over the cutout shapes, and hold in place with two spots of rubber cement on the top corners of the paper (Ill. 2).
4. Cut out shapes and rubber cement these for the middle ground of the original drawing on the above translucent paper (Ill. 3).
5. Cover this with another translucent paper and hold it in place with rubber cement on the top corners.
6. Complete the picture by rubber cementing objects on the top of the translucent paper (Ill. 4).

NOTE: As long as the first silhouette is visible through the translucent paper, the procedure can be continued. Translucent paper which is too heavy reduces the number of silhouettes. Designs cut from colored cellophane and placed between translucent paper make interesting transparent window decorations.

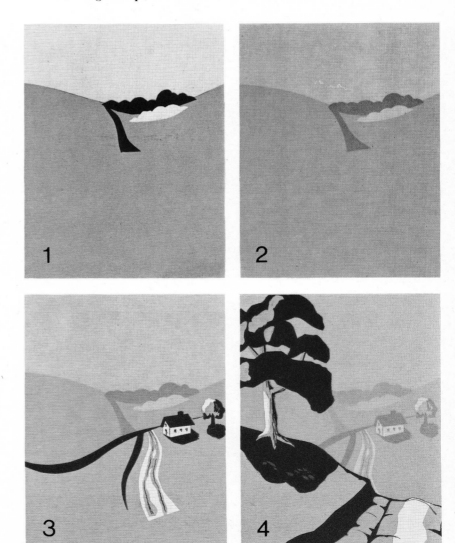

1

2

3

Geometric Design

Supplies

1. Colored paper
2. Scissors
3. Paste

Procedure

1. Cut geometric shapes which are varied in size and color. Cutting some of these shapes into halves or quarters not only offers more variety of shapes but correlates well with the teaching of fractions.
2. Group a number of geometric shapes together until they form a picture.
3. When satisfied with the arrangement, paste the shapes in place on background paper.

Letter Collé

A collé is a technique invented by the early cubists in which scraps of paper are pasted to the canvas to provide decorative and tactile embellishments.

Procedure

1. Select a number of magazine letters of various sizes and colors.
2. Cut out selected letters.
3. Combine two or more letters to create figures, scenes or a design.
4. Arrange this group of letters on a piece of background paper.
5. Paste the letters in place when satisfied.

Supplies

1. Colored magazine letters to be used as texture
2. Scissors
3. Paste
4. Sheet of white or colored paper for background

Magazine Collé

A collé is a technique invented by the early cubists in which scraps of paper are pasted to the canvas to provide decorative and tactile embellishments.

Supplies

1. Colored magazine pictures to be used as texture
2. Scissors
3. Paste
4. Sheet of white or colored paper for background

Procedure

1. Select a number of magazine pictures containing areas which may be used for textural effects.
2. Cut these areas into shapes which, when combined, will create a scene or design.
3. Arrange these paper shapes on background paper.
4. Paste the paper shapes in place when satisfied.

NOTE: Do not use the texture to create the subject matter from which it came—instead adapt it to other uses, i.e., an illustration of cornflakes could be cut to represent a plowed field, hay stack, rumpled hair, etc.

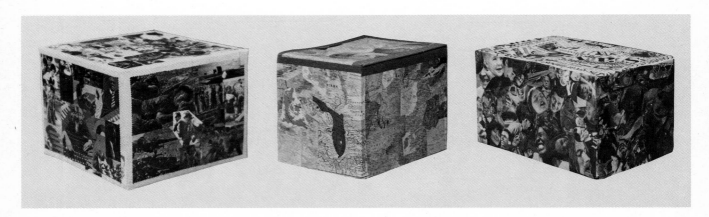

Mat Board—Cut and Peel

Procedure

1. Cut lightly into the surface and around each shape that has been previously drawn on colored mat board.
2. Peel out each area after it has been cut.
3. Contrasting color areas can be added with colored paper, paint, or crayon.

Supplies

1. Cutting tool (single-edge razor blade or sharp knife)
2. Colored mat board

Paper Bag Mask

Supplies

1. Paper bag large enough to slip over child's head
2. Scissors
3. Rubber cement, paste, or glue, and a stapler, if one is available
4. Watercolors, tempera paint, or colored inks
5. Materials to be used for decorating mask, such as bits of colored paper, felt or cloth, bottle caps, buttons, yarn, ribbons, etc.
6. Paint brush and container for water, if paint is used

Procedure

1. Slip the bag over the child's head. The *bottom* of the bag will be the *top* of the mask. You may need to cut out sections at the sides of the bag so that it will fit more comfortably over the shoulders.
2. Locate the eyes and mark them with a blunt crayon. Remove the bag and cut the openings for the eyes. Add the nose, mouth, and, if you wish, ears.
3. Decorate the bag with any of the media and materials listed above.

Paper Bag Puppet

Procedure

1. Put hand in the paper bag with the index finger touching the top.
2. Spread the thumb and the second finger and make a small hole in the side of the bag where fingers touch. These holes are necessary to control and manipulate the puppet.
3. Features that have been cut out can now be stapled or glued in place.

Supplies

1. Paper bag, the size to be determined by the size of the hand (only large enough to get hand in)
2. Construction paper (colored)
3. Rubber cement, paste, or stapler

Paper Bag Puppet on a Stick

Supplies

1. Paper bag
2. Newspapers
3. Wooden stick or dowel
4. String
5. Colored paper and scissors
6. Paints or crayons
7. Paste

Procedure

1. Fill the bag with small pieces of torn or shredded newspaper.
2. The dowel or stick should be inserted in the open end of the bag, and until it touches the bottom of the bag. Gather the open end of the bag around the stick, and tie the string tightly to form a neck. Make sure the stick extends far enough out of the bag to made a handle.
3. The features of the face can be added with paint, crayons, or with pieces of colored paper cut to shape.

   NOTE: Faces or animals can be cut from paper and mounted to a stick; they also make simple puppet heads.

Paper Finger Puppet

Procedure

1. Cut a strip of paper to form a tube that will fit the finger snugly. A small paper tube will also work.
2. Tape or paste the tube together.
3. Add features with paper, paint, crayons, felt tip pens, or by cutting or folding the paper tube itself.

NOTE: Finger puppets can also be created from the fingers cut from an old glove and decorated. Try a paper cup with an opening cut for the nose through which a finger is protruded. A paper plate folded in half to form a large mouth and decorated has possibilities.

Supplies

1. Paper
2. Paste or white glue
3. Tape
4. Scissors
5. Paint, crayons, felt markers

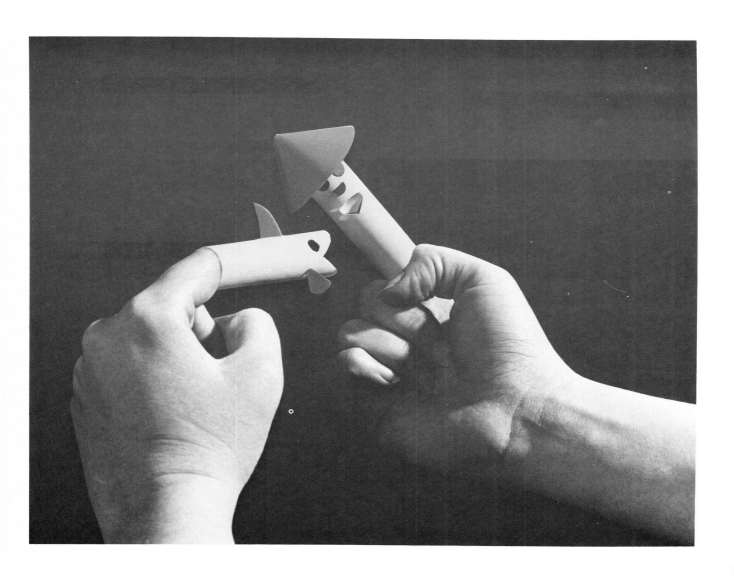

Paper Mosaic

A mosaic is a design made by the close placement of small pieces of colored material. Historically mosaics can be traced back to classical antiquity. They were composed of small pieces of colored glass or stones imbedded in a binding agent.

Supplies

1. Scissors
2. Colored paper scraps or colored magazine pictures
3. Paste or rubber cement
4. Corsage or hat pin (for lifting pieces of paper)
5. Pencil
6. Background paper

Procedure

1. Make a light pencil drawing on the background paper.
2. Cut the colored paper into small fairly uniform sizes—try to keep the pieces sorted by color to save time later when pasting.
3. Apply the paste to the individual pieces and place them on the drawing. Leave a narrow space of background color between the pieces of paper. A corsage pin will help in picking up the bits of paper.
4. Continue pasting until the design is completed.

NOTE: Other interesting mosaics can be made with confetti, seeds, grain, punched paper bits, etc.

Paper Script Design

Procedure

1. Fold the paper in half.
2. Write a word or name in script with a crayon along the creased edge. The crayon is used to insure enough thickness of line to permit the cutting of letters on both sides.
3. Cut on both sides of the crayoned line, making sure each letter is held together by the fold.
4. Paste the letters which have been cut out on contrasting colored paper. Additional cut paper may be added to develop a suggested image.

NOTE: A word containing a letter which extends below the line (such as f, g, j, p, q, y) must be written above the fold so only the extension of that letter reaches the fold. View the accompanying illustrations from the side in order to see the original name from which the design was created.

Supplies

1. Scissors
2. Paper
3. Paste
4. Crayon

Paper Strip Picture

Supplies

1. Colored construction paper
2. Rubber cement or library paste
3. Scissors
4. Clear tape

Procedure

1. Cut the colored construction paper into ¼ or ½ inch strips.
2. Form the strips into numerous shapes, fastening the ends together with paste or clear tape if necessary.
3. Choose a number of various shapes and place them on contrasting colored paper to form a design or picture.
4. When satisfied with the arrangement and color, place a small amount of paste or rubber cement on one edge of the form and fasten in place.

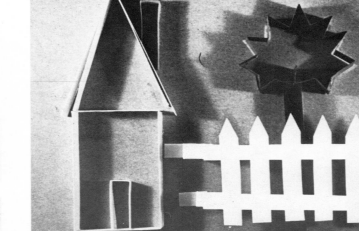

Paper Textures

The flat surface of a piece of paper can be changed into a textured surface by many methods, five of which are suggested below. Also see paper sculpture, pages 207-209.

Procedure

Method A

Cut or slit a paper with cutting instrument and push the shapes out from the back. Be sure to place a piece of cardboard under the work when cutting.

Supplies

1. Paper
2. Scissors, knife, or single-edge razor blade
3. Paste, rubber cement, or white glue
4. Piece of cardboard (to be placed under work when cutting)

Method B

Form numerous small three-dimensional paper shapes of various colors and fasten to a piece of paper in a contrasting color to form a texture picture.

A

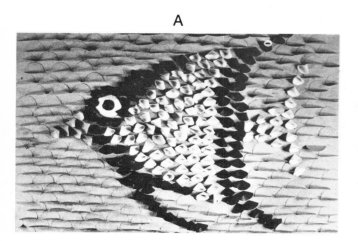

Enlargement of A

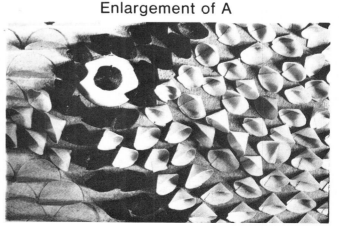

Method C
Curled paper strips fastened close together on a piece of paper will also create an interesting texture.

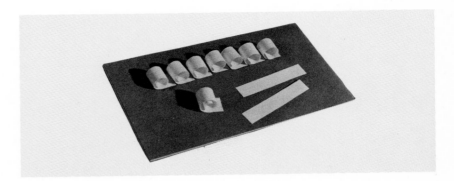

Method D
Strips of paper with one edge cut in a decorative manner and the other edge folded to a right angle, and then fastened close together on a base paper, create interesting textures.

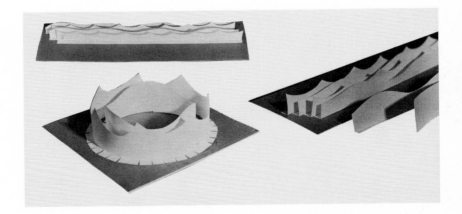

Method E
Scoring and folding a flat sheet of paper will create numerous three-dimensional textures. Scoring is achieved by pressure with a comparatively dull, smooth instrument (closed scissors, metal file, etc.) drawn across the paper in order to dent the paper so it can be folded more easily. After folding and creasing the paper on the scored lines, it can be opened and forced into lowered and raised creases.

Paper Weaving

Procedure

1. Cut a series of slits in the paper, making sure a border is maintained.
2. Cut strips of colored paper, magazines, wallpaper, etc.
3. Weave the strips through the slits in the paper.
4. Hold strips in place with a spot of paste if necessary.

NOTE: Numerous designs can be obtained through an inventive approach. The paper can be folded in half to cut a series of slits, as shown.

Supplies

1. Paper
2. Scissors
3. Paste

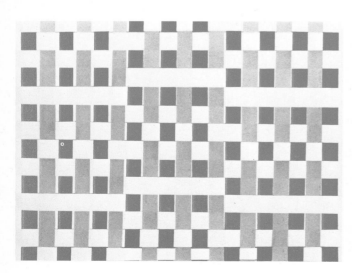

Positive and Negative Design

Supplies

1. Colored paper
2. Paste or rubber cement
3. Scissors

Procedure

Method A

This is the simpler procedure of the two and the one most appropriate for young children.

1. Select one sheet of colored paper (Ill. 1) and one-half sheet of a contrasting color (Ill. 2).

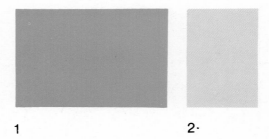

1   2·

2. Fold the small sheet in half (Ill. 3).
3. Cut a design directly out of the folded side (Ill. 4) (a pencil drawing may be helpful in cutting out the design). The section cut out is the positive (Ill. 6) and the section containing the opening is the negative part (Ill. 5) of the design.

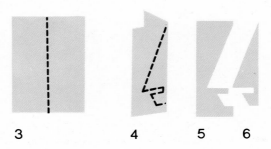

3   4   5   6

4. Unfold both parts, laying the negative section (Ill. 7) on the uncut sheet of contrasting color paper, squaring it up on one end. Paste in place.
5. Place the positive section (Ill. 8) on the other half of the uncut sheet and paste it in place.

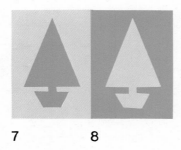

7   8

6. To carry a design further, cut both the positive (Ill. 9) and negative (Ill. 10) pieces on the fold.
7. Alternate the positive and negative pieces and paste on contrasting colored paper (Ill. 11).

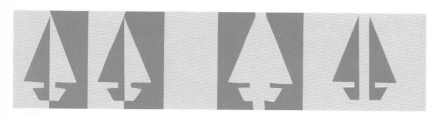

11   Negative 10   Positive 9

Method B. An allover pattern.

1. Select one sheet of colored paper (Ill. 1) and one-half sheet of a contrasting color (Ill. 2).

1   2

2. Cut the smaller sheet into four or eight equal parts (Ill. 3).

3   4

3. Fold one part in half and cut a design directly from the folded edge (Ill. 4) (a pencil drawing may be helpful in cutting out the design). The section cut out is the positive, and the section containing the opening is the negative part of the design.

   If the allover pattern is to be repeated in every respect (color and design), fold the remaining parts in half and lay the negative piece over each part in turn. Trace the design with a pencil, then cut out each part along the pencil line.
4. Unfold all of the positive and negative sections and cut along each fold so that each section is divided into two parts.
5. Paste one-half of the negative part in the upper left–hand corner of the full sheet (Ill. 5).
6. Paste one-half of the positive part so the original design is completed.
7. The allover pattern can be completed by alternating the positive and negative sections until all the sections are used and the paper is filled.

5

NOTE: Many variations and allover patterns can be created by changing designs and color. In a pure positive-negative design, no scraps will be left over.

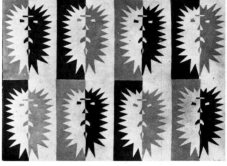

The above design is not a repeated, but an *assembled* design.

Swirl Paper

Supplies

1. Powder paint or oil paint
2. Large vessel containing water (a wide shallow container such as a photographic tray is best)
3. Paper
4. Small vessels for color mixing
5. Turpentine
6. Soap or detergent
7. Paper towels or cloths

Procedure

1. Pour a small quantity of turpentine into the mixing vessel, and add enough powder paint, or oil paint, to bring it to the desired color strength.
2. Pour the colored turpentine on the surface of the water in the large vessel.
3. Stir the water, thereby exciting the turpentine into interesting patterns.
4. Pick up the color patterns with the paper. In doing this the paper may be dropped on, or dragged across, the surface of the water. A little experimentation will demonstrate that various methods of color pickup may be used in obtaining the desired effects.
5. Cleanse the containers, using soap or detergent, and cloths or paper towels.

NOTE: If multicolored designs are desired they may be created by adding more than one color to the water and the container, or by dipping one color at a time until several are combined. Although spontaneity is the most interesting feature of swirl paper, it should be pointed out that it is possible to achieve a degree of control over the patterns. Portions of the patterns may be placed where desired by simply touching certain areas of the paper to the water.

Swirl papers are a great stimulant for the imagination. Many things may be read into the pattern and these may be made more visible by adding chalk, crayon, or ink.

Swirl papers may be used decoratively as a covering for such objects as notebooks, wastebaskets, boxes, etc.

Three-Dimensional Picture or Poster

Procedure

1. Cut the subjects from a drawing or painting.
2. Make a number of small cardboard stilts of various sizes and paste them on the back of each cutout. A narrow strip of cardboard folded into a square shape and fastened with a piece of tape makes an ideal stilt.
3. Paste each cutout on background paper, making sure that any subject which is meant to appear close to the viewer projects higher from the paper than those meant to be in the distance.

NOTE: Many other methods of creating a three-dimensional effect in paper can be improvised after a little experimentation.

Supplies

1. Colored construction paper
2. Pencil
3. Scissors
4. Paste, glue, or tape

Torn Paper Picture

Supplies

1. Colored paper
2. Scissors
3. Paste

Procedure

1. Determine the subject to be treated and tear the paper into shapes adaptable to the subject.
2. Arrange these torn shapes on a piece of paper that will serve as a background.
3. Paste each piece in place to complete the picture.

NOTE: Drawing can be added to provide detail.

PRINTING PROCESSES

Cardboard or Rubber Block Print

Supplies

1. A piece of inner tube or cardboard
2. Scissors
3. Paste or glue
4. Heavy cardboard, floor tile, or a piece of wood
5. Water-soluble or oil base printers' ink
6. Brayer (roller)
7. Ink slab (9″ x 9″ floor tile, or a piece of glass with taped edges to prevent cutting fingers)
8. Paper
9. Newspaper
10. Turpentine, benzine, carbon tetrachloride, or kerosene for cleaning the brayer, inking slab, and printing block if oil base printers's ink is used

Procedure

1. Cut shapes from pieces of cardboard or inner tubes and glue them to a cardboard background for printing.
2. Squeeze a small amount of ink from the tube onto the piece of glass or floor tile.
3. Roll the ink with a brayer until it is spread smoothly on the inking slab (see Ill. 1).
4. Roll the ink brayer over the mounted design from side to side and top to bottom to insure an even distribution over the entire surface.
5. Place a piece of paper over the inked design and rub gently and evenly with the fingers, or with a smooth bottom of a small jar until the entire design is reproduced. It would be wise to peel back a corner of the paper to determine whether further rubbing is necessary for a strong print (see Ill. 2).
6. Re-ink the design for subsequent prints.

Cork Print

Procedure

1. Use the cutting tool to cut a design around the edge and/or the middle of the cork.
2. Place a pad of newspapers under the paper to be printed. Have a scrap paper or paper towel available on which to try the design and to ascertain whether or not too much paint is being used.
3. Cover the surface of the cork with paint and print on a scrap of paper to eliminate any excess paint. One or two prints may be tried on the scrap paper so that too much paint is not being used. Printing may now begin. A single application of paint will serve for three or four printings, and these may be combined to make an overall pattern.
4. Several different colors may be applied. If these are also applied to different areas of the cork, interesting prints may result.

Supplies

1. Cork
2. Single-edge razor blade or penknife
3. Paper
4. Tempera paint
5. Brush

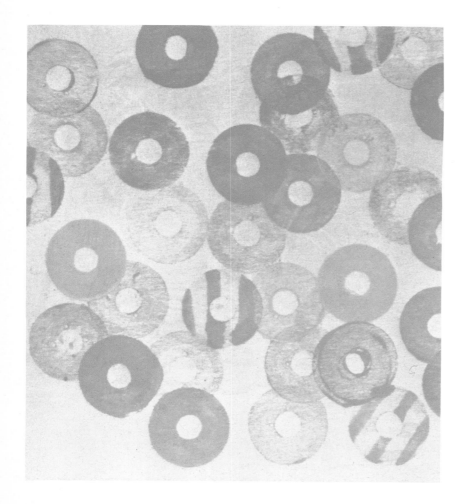

Crayon Print

Supplies

1. Wax crayon
2. Typing paper
3. Turpentine or mineral spirits
4. Cloth or paper towel
5. Piece of window screen

Procedure

1. Draw heavily with the crayon on a piece of paper which has been placed over a piece of window screen. The screen merely assumes a thick covering of crayon.
2. Spread a thin coat of turpentine or mineral spirits on the back to soften the wax.
3. When the wax is softened, lay a piece of paper over the illustration and rub with your fingers or a flat tool until the picture is transferred. It may be possible to produce several prints from one drawing.

NOTE: Also see crayon shavings print, page 177.

Original

Print

Crayon Shavings Print

Procedure

1. Shave the pieces of scrap crayon on a piece of newspaper, breaking them up into particles no larger than pinheads.
2. Place the crayon particles in a clean, dry salt shaker.
3. Sprinkle a few of the crayon shavings on a piece of white paper which is then placed on a piece of newspaper.
4. Place a piece of foil over the crayon particles.
5. Press over the foil with a moderately hot iron.
6. Remove the foil and place it on a second sheet of paper and press once again. Separate the foil from the white paper, which has received the printed impression.

NOTE: Color areas may be controlled using separate shakers containing special colors or the variegated colors may be given definite shapes through the use of cut stencils. See instructions on cutting a stencil, pages 222–23. Also see crayon printing on page 176.

Supplies

1. Scrap pieces of crayon
2. Scraping tool (nail file, scissors, etc.)
3. Aluminum foil
4. Paper
5. Salt shaker
6. Iron
7. Newspapers

Finger Paint Mono-Print

Supplies

1. Finger paints
2. Smooth flat surface (piece of glass with edges taped to prevent cut fingers, table top, etc.)
3. Paper
4. Newspaper
5. Iron

Procedure

1. Do a finger painting directly on the table top or other smooth flat surface.
2. Lay a piece of paper directly on the wet painting and rub with the hand until the painting is transferred to the paper.
3. Lift the painting and place on the newspaper to dry.
4. When the print has dried, place it face down on a flat surface and press with a warm iron.

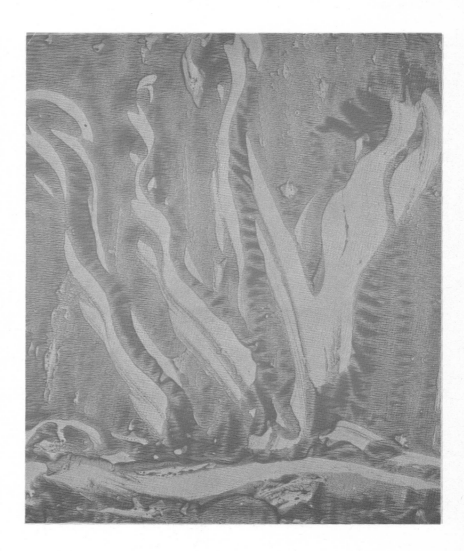

Ink Pad Print

Procedure

1. Place a pad of newspapers under the paper to be printed.
2. Press a finger, heel of hand, side of hand or any item to be printed on the ink pad.
3. Press the inked area to the printing paper. One application of ink should serve for several impressions, which can be combined to make an overall pattern.

NOTE: Sticks, jar lids, pencil erasers, or any small flat item may make an interesting printing tool.

Supplies

1. Paper
2. Ink pad
3. Newspapers

Linoleum Block Print

Supplies

1. Battleship linoleum (heavy linoleum)
2. Carving tools (V- or U-shaped gouges set in wooden handles, penknife, etc.) Cutting tools are available which are drawn toward you. These reduce the risk of small children cutting themselves.
3. Paper
4. Carbon paper
5. Water-soluble or oil base printers' ink
6. Brayer (roller)
7. Ink slab (9" x 9" floor tile or piece of glass with taped edges to prevent cut fingers)
8. Newspapers
9. Turpentine, carbon tetrachloride, benzine, or kerosene for cleaning glass, brayer, and linoleum block, if oil base printers' ink is used

Procedure

1. Cut the linoleum to the desired size and plan the design on a sheet of paper of equal dimensions.
2. Transfer the design from the paper to the linoleum with carbon paper and sharp pencil. If lettering is incorporated in the design, it must be carved in reverse.
3. Carve the design in the linoleum by cutting away all lines or areas which are not to be printed. Warm the linoleum for easier cutting. Keep the hand which holds the linoleum out of the path of the cutting tool. (See supply list for salt tools).
4. Check the design from time to time by placing a thin piece of paper over the carving and rubbing over the surface with a crayon or pencil.
5. Squeeze a small amount of ink from the tube onto the ink slab.
6. Roll the ink with the brayer until it is spread smoothly on the inking slab.
7. Roll the ink brayer over the carved linoleum design until it is completely and evenly covered.
8. Print.

   a. Lay a piece of paper on which the printing is to be done over several thicknesses of newspaper. Place the ink block face down on the paper—cover with another piece of paper to keep clean and print by pressing down firmly with the hand or foot. Tapping with a mallet is also a good method.

   b. Place a piece of paper over the inked design and rub gently and evenly with the fingers or the smooth bottom of a small jar until the entire design is reproduced. It would be wise to peel back a corner of the paper to determine whether further rubbing is necessary for a strong print (see illustrations).

9. Re-ink the linoleum block for subsequent prints.

   NOTE: The quality of the print may be improved by soaking the paper briefly in water and blotting the surface prior to printing if oil base ink is used.

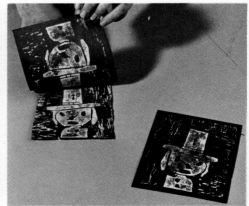

Paint Mono-Print

Procedure

1. Paint a design directly on a non-absorbent surface. Keep design simple with large colored areas. Allow to dry.
2. Thoroughly dampen sheet of drawing paper.
3. Press the dampened paper firmly and evenly over the painted design with the palm of the hand.
4. Carefully peel the paper from the design.
5. A single impression printing will appear on the paper as a mirror image.

Supplies

1. Smooth non-absorbent hard surface (glass, plastic, table top, etc.)
2. Drawing paper
3. Tempera paint
4. Brush
5. Water container

Original

Print

Plaster Block Print

Supplies

1. Modeling plaster
2. Ink slab (9″ x 9″ floor tile, or a piece of glass with taped edges to prevent cut fingers)
3. Plastic clay (plastilene)
4. Shellac and brush
5. Carving tools (V- or U-shaped gouges set in wooden handles, penknife, nail, hairpin, orange stick, etc.)
6. Thin paper
7. Water-soluble or oil base printers' ink
8. Brayer (roller)
9. Turpentine, carbon tetrachloride, benzine, or kerosene for cleaning brayer, ink slab, and plaster block, if oil base ink is used
10. A second piece of glass is advised, for it will provide a perfectly smooth surface on which to pour the plaster

Procedure

1. Build a wall of clay on a piece of glass to the desired shape and area. This will be the plaster mold.
2. Mix the plaster. (See pages 198–99.)
3. Pour the plaster into the mold and allow it to dry.
4. Remove the clay wall and slide the plaster block from the glass and the plaster to harden further.
5. Brush the surface of the plaster with shellac to give it a surface color through which the cuts can be seen.
6. Plan a design to fit the cast plaster shape.
7. Transfer the design to the plaster block with carbon paper by retracing the lines with a pencil.
8. Carve the design in the plaster block with any suitable tool. Cut away all areas or lines which are not to be printed.
9. Squeeze a small amount of ink from the tube onto the piece of glass or floor tile.
10. Roll the ink with a brayer until it is spread smoothly on the inking slab.
11. Roll the ink brayer over the carved plaster design from side to side and top to bottom to insure an even distribution over the entire surface.
12. Place a piece of paper over the inked design and rub it gently and evenly with the fingers or the smooth bottom of a small jar until the entire design is reproduced. It will be wise to peel back a corner of the paper to determine whether further rubbing is necessary for a strong print.
13. Re-ink the plaster design for subsequent prints. Two or three dozen impressions can be made if the plaster block is handled carefully.

NOTE: The quality of the print may be improved by soaking the paper briefly in water and blotting the surface prior to printing if oil base ink is used.

Potato Print

Procedure

1. Cut the potato in half so that each surface is *flat*. If a large potato is used, it may be cut into several pieces, but each piece must be large, so that it will not break in printing.
2. Young children may incise or scratch the design into the surface of the potato with a nail file, pencil, or other tools.
3. Cut around the edge of the design to approximately ⅛ inch in depth. Then remove the background by cutting to the design from the outer edge of the potato.
4. Place a pad of newspapers under the paper to be printed. Have a scrap paper or paper towel available on which to try the design and to ascertain whether or not too much paint is being used.
5. Cover the surface of the design with paint and print on a scrap of paper to eliminate any excess paint. One or two prints may be tried on the scrap paper so that too much paint is not being used. The texture of the potato should be transferred for more interesting prints. Printing may now be continued. A single application of paint will serve for three or four printings, and these may be combined to make an overall pattern.
6. Several different colors may be applied. If these are also applied to different areas of the potato, interesting prints will result. The water contained in the potato will make the colors blend and run, producing more colorful designs.

NOTE: Carrots, turnips, cabbage, etc., also may be used for successful printing. This process may be employed to make attractive wrapping paper, Christmas cards, program covers, decorations, place cards, etc.

Supplies

1. Solid potato
2. A scratching tool (pencil, nail file, comb, nail, scissors, or orange stick). Small children may work satisfactorily with these tools without the dangers involved in the use of sharply edged tools.
3. A sharply edged cutting tool, such as a paring knife or pocketknife
4. Colored construction paper, drawing paper, tissue paper, brown wrapping paper, manila paper, or newsprint
5. Paint brush
6. Water jar
7. Watercolors, tempera paint, or finger paint
8. Tray for mixing colors
9. Absorbent cloth

Screen Print

Supplies

1. Embroidery hoop, or small wooden picture frame
2. A piece of material large enough to cover the hoop or frame—dotted swiss, cheese cloth, etc.
3. Stapler
4. Stencil paper (the back of typewriter stencil serves as a most satisfactory and inexpensive paper)
5. Squeegee (tongue depressor, small piece of linoleum with a straight edge, small plastic windshield scraper, etc.)
6. Paper
7. Cutting tool (scissors, knife, single-edge razor blade)
8. Finger paint or commercial screen process ink (other paints clog the pores of the cloth). A good, inexpensive silk screen paint can be made by mixing liquid or instant powder tempera with a stiff mixture of soap flakes (not detergent) and warm water, or with a media mixer.

Procedure

1. Using two or three layers, stretch the material tightly between the embroidery hoops. If a wooden frame is used, tightly stretch the material and staple it in place.
2. Cut the design from the stencil paper (Ill. 1), using paper which is a bit larger than the surface of the stretched material. The cut design must fit within the area of the stretched material. The stencil should be cut following the directions on pages 222 and 223.
3. Place a piece of paper on a flat and smooth surface.
4. Place the stencil on the paper (Ill. 2).
5. Place the screen on top of the stencil (Ill. 3). Make sure the material is in contact with the stencil to prevent the paint from running under the stencil.
6. Place some commercial screening paint, or finger paint of tooth paste consistency, in the frame or hoop (Ill. 4).

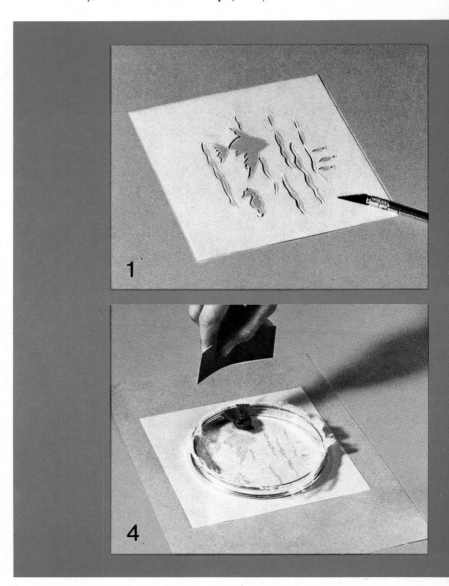

7. Hold the frame with one hand and scrape the paint across the stencil with a squeegee. In this process, the paint or ink is forced through the cloth and adheres the stencil to the screen, except where the design was cut out, and these areas will be reproduced (Ill. 5).
8. Gently lift the stencil and frame, making sure the stencil remains adhered to the material (Ill. 6).
9. Place the frame and stencil on another paper and repeat step six and step seven for additional prints. Work rapidly to prevent paint from drying and clogging the material.

NOTE: Lines and shapes may be created in this print by using crayon as a resist. The drawing should be done with the crayon directly on the material in the screen.

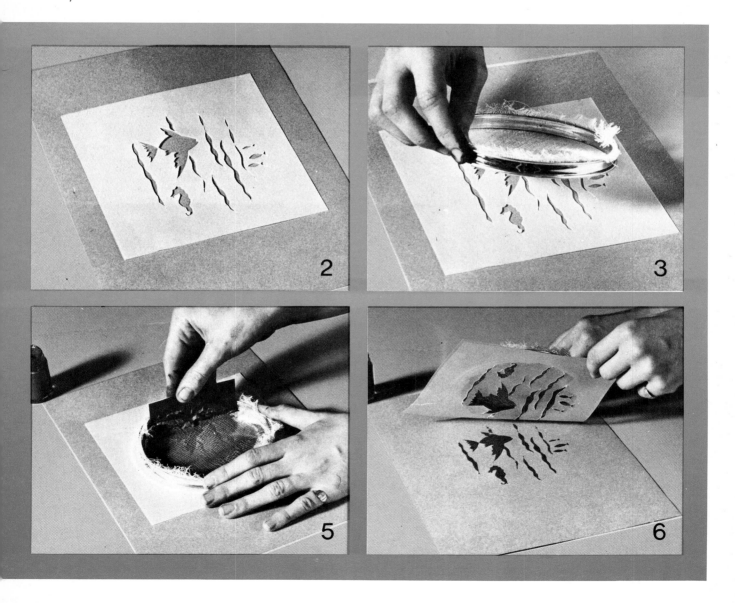

Soap Block Print

Supplies

1. Large bar of soap
2. Carving tool (nail, scissors, knife, orange stick, etc.)
3. Straight-edge scraper for smoothing surface of the soap (table knife)
4. Oil base printers' ink
5. Brayer (roller)
6. Ink slab (9″ x 9″ floor tile, or a piece of glass with taped edges to prevent cut fingers)
7. Paper
8. Turpentine, carbon tetrachloride, benzine, or kerosene for cleaning brayer, ink slab, and soap design, if oil base printers' ink is used

Procedure

1. Smooth one side of the bar of soap with a straight-edge scraper. Make sure any design or trade-mark is removed and the surface is flat.
2. Plan a design on thin paper the size of the smooth surface of the soap.
3. Transfer the design from the paper to the smooth surface of the soap by tracing over the drawing with a sharp pencil.
4. Carve the design into the soap by cutting away all lines or areas which are not to be printed.
5. Check the design from time to time by placing the thin piece of paper over the carving and rubbing over the surface with a crayon or pencil.
6. Squeeze a small amount of ink from the tube onto the ink slab.
7. Roll the ink with a brayer until it is spread smoothly on the inking slab.
8. Roll the ink brayer over the carved soap design from side to side, top to bottom, to insure an even distribution over the entire surface.
9. Place a piece of paper over the inked design and rub gently and evenly with the fingers or the smooth bottom of a small jar until the entire design is reproduced. It would be wise to peel back a corner of the paper to determine if further rubbing is necessary for a strong print.
10. Re-ink the soap design for subsequent prints.

NOTE: Avoid too much pressure when printing to prevent distortion of the printing surface.

Sponge Print

Procedure

1. Cut pieces of sponge into various shapes and sizes.
2. Mix the desired number of colors in the small lids or dishes. (The mixture can be one of water and tempera paint, or liquid starch and tempera paint.)
3. Dip the sponges into the colors and print by pressing lightly onto the paper.

Supplies

1. Sponge
2. Dry or liquid tempera paint
3. Scissors
4. Water container
5. Paper
6. Starch (liquid)
7. Small dishes or lids

Stamps for Printing

Supplies

1. String
2. Glue
3. Block of wood
4. Paper
5. Tempera paint or water-soluble block-printing ink
6. Brush

Procedure

1. Deposit a small quantity of glue on a newspaper or paper towel.
2. Rub one side of the block in the glue to produce a thin coating.
3. Place the string in the glue on the block so as to form the design and allow the glue to dry.
4. Lightly press the string into the ink or paint which has been spread out on a smooth surface.
5. Print:

   a. Lay the printing paper over several thicknesses of newspaper.
   b. Press the string on a scrap of paper to eliminate any excess paint.
   c. Several prints can now be made on the printing paper before applying more paint.

NOTE: The string may be removed and replaced in the form of a different design for new prints. Instead of painting the design, a print may also be obtained by stamping on an ink pad.

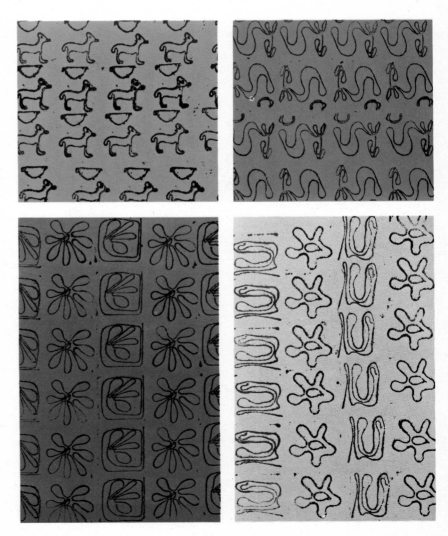

Stick Print

Procedure

1. Make a light pencil drawing on paper.
2. Cut a number of sticks of different sizes and shapes, 2 or 3 inches long, making sure the ends are cut square.
3. Mix a small amount of paint on a piece of nonabsorbent scrap paper and smooth it with a brush to an even consistency.
4. Dip the stick in the film of paint.
5. Press the stick to a scrap of paper and print one or two images to remove any excess paint.
6. Now press the stick to the drawing which has been placed on a pad of newspaper and repeat until the image becomes too light.
7. Repeat process four until design is completed.
8. A mosaic effect is obtainable by leaving a narrow space of background paper between each individual print; overlapping individual prints and colors also create interesting effects. One may also try twisting the stick when printing.

NOTE: Angle irons, jar lids, matchbox folders, etc., are also possible printing tools. Unusual patterns may be created by dipping the edges of any of the above in paint.

Supplies

1. Small sticks, two to three inches long, of various sizes and shapes
2. Tempera or latex paint
3. Brush
4. Paper
5. Pad of newspaper

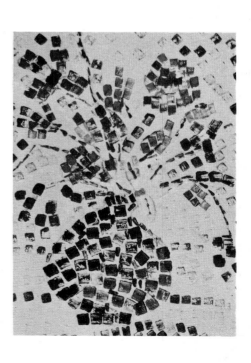

Styrofoam Print

Supplies

1. Pieces of styrofoam
2. Cutting tool (sharp knife or single-edge razor blade)
3. Paper
4. Tempera paint
5. Brush
6. Water container
7. Mixing tray

Procedure

1. Cut the styrofoam in various shapes, making sure each printing surface is flat.
2. Designs may be incised (scratched) into the surface of the styrofoam with a pencil, nail file, scissors or other similar tool.
3. Place a pad of newspapers under the paper to be printed. Have a scrap paper or paper towel available on which to try the design and to ascertain whether or not too much paint is being used.
4. Cover the surface of the design with paint and print on a scrap of paper to eliminate any excess paint. One or two prints may be tried on the scrap paper so that too much paint is not being used. The texture of the styrofoam should be transferred for more interesting prints. A single application of paint will serve for three or four printings, and these may be combined to make an overall pattern.
5. Several different colors may be applied. If these are also applied to different areas of the styrofoam, interesting prints will result.

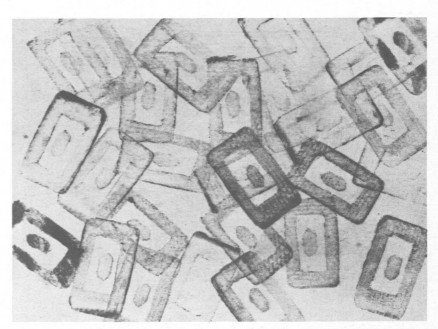

Texture Mono-Print

Procedure

1. Cover piece of construction paper with a coating of wax crayons.
2. Using a paper towel, buff the crayoned paper until smooth. This process should prevent the paper from curling.
3. Place approximately two or three heaping tablespoons of media mixer onto the buffed crayon surface.
4. Into the media mixer blend a selected color of paint.
5. This colored mixture should be quite heavy, the consistency of cake icing.
6. Place another piece of paper on top of the layer of mixed media.
7. Use the finger tips to lightly smooth the paper—do not press too heavily.
8. Pull the print from the base paper.
9. Repeat the process several times with differently colored paint.

Supplies

1. Construction paper
2. Crayons
3. Prang Media Mixer (see Formulas and Hints)
4. Tempera (liquid or powder)

Wood-block Print

Supplies

1. Soft piece of pine wood
2. Carving tools (V- or U-shaped gouges set in wooden handles, pen-knife, etc.) Tools are available which can be drawn toward you. These eliminate the possibility of cut fingers.
3. Paper
4. Carbon paper
5. Water-soluble or oil base printers' ink
6. Brayer (roller)
7. Ink slab (9″ x 9″ floor tile, or a piece of glass with taped edges to prevent cut fingers)
8. Newspapers
9. Turpentine, carbon tetrachloride, benzine, or kerosene for cleaning brayer, ink slab, and wood block, if oil base printers' ink is used

Procedure

1. Plan a design on paper to fit the wood-block size, deciding on which areas are to be cut away or left in relief.
2. Transfer the design from the paper to the wooden block with carbon paper and a sharp pencil. If lettering is to be incorporated in the design, it must be carved in reverse.
3. Carve the design in the wood block. Cut away all the lines or areas which are not to be printed. In carving the wood, all cuts should be made in the direction of the grain. Cross-grain cuts will bind the tool and splinter the wood. Keep the hand which holds the wooden block out of the path of the cutting tool. (See "Supplies" for draw tools.)
4. Check the design from time to time by placing a thin piece of paper over the carving and rubbing over the surface with a crayon or pencil.
5. Squeeze a small amount of ink from the tube onto the piece of glass or floor tile.
6. Roll the ink with the brayer until it is spread smoothly on the inking slab.
7. Roll the ink brayer over the carved wood block design until it is completely and evenly covered.
8. Print.

   a. Lay a piece of paper on which the printing is to be done over several thicknesses of newspaper. Place the inked block face down on the paper—cover with a piece of paper to keep clean and print

by pressing down firmly with the hand or foot. Tapping with a mallet is also a good method.

b. Place a piece of paper over the inked design and rub gently and evenly with the fingers, spoon or smooth bottom of small jar until entire design is reproduced. It would be wise to peel back a corner of the paper to determine whether further rubbing is necessary for a strong print.

9. Re-ink the wood block for subsequent prints.

NOTE: If one decides to make use of the decorative advantages of the grain of the wood, he or she may make this grain printable by soaking the wood in water so that the grain stands out in relief. If only certain areas of the grain are to be used, the remainder of the block may be sealed with shellac and the exposed area soaked with water. Too much soaking will cause the block to warp or buckle. Brushing with a stiff wire brush will also expose the grain.

The block may also be given textures by scratching the surface with various types of abrasives or tools, or by striking patterns with chisels, screwdrivers, etc.

The quality of the print may be improved by soaking the paper briefly in water and blotting the surface prior to printing if oil base ink is used.

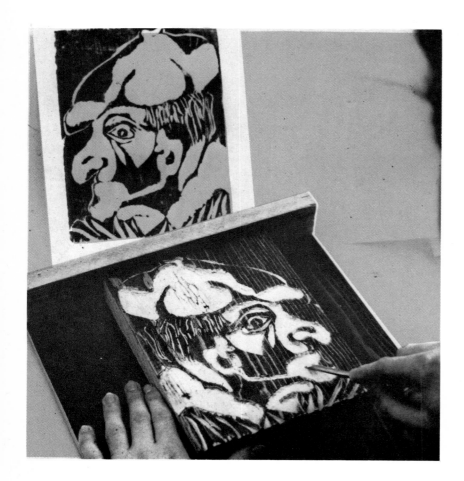

Wood-block and String Print

Supplies

1. Wooden block
2. String
3. Paste or glue
4. Paper
5. Tempera paint
6. Brush

Procedure

1. Coat the entire length of the string with paste or glue.
2. While the string is still wet with the paste or the glue, wrap it around the wooden block to form a design.
3. Place a small amount of tempera paint on a piece of scrap paper and smooth it with a brush to an even consistency.
4. Choose the side of the string-wrapped block which has the most pleasing design and dip it in the film of paint, or merely apply the paint to the string with a brush.
5. Lift the block from the paint and press it against the paper with some pressure. Several prints can be made before applying more paint. It is suggested that the first impression be made on scrap paper to eliminate any excess paint.

NOTE: Many interesting allover patterns can be printed by alternating the various sides of the block.

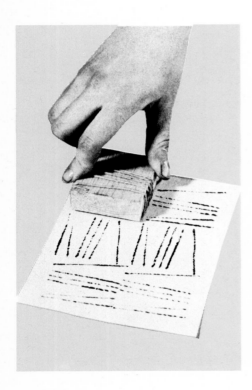

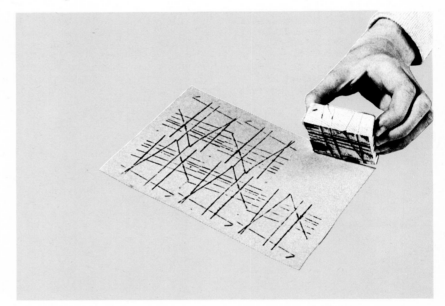

SCULPTURE

Box Sculpture

Supplies

1. Assortment of cardboard, wooden or metal containers (oatmeal boxes, hat boxes, coffee tins, jewelry boxes, cartons, etc.)
2. Miscellaneous materials (colored paper, string, etc.)
3. Glue, rubber cement or tape
4. Scissors
5. Paint (tempera, latex)
6. Brush

Procedure

1. Containers such as those suggested above, when combined with miscellaneous materials, lend themselves to the construction of animals, figures, totem poles, hats, percussion instruments, etc.

Bread Dough Sculpture

Procedure

1. Remove the crusts from four slices of bread.
2. Tear the bread into small pieces, mixing them thoroughly with three tablespoons of white glue and one-to-two drops of lemon juice.
3. Model or cut as desired, allowing one-to-two days for complete drying.
4. Pieces may be painted with watercolor, tempera, or acrylic paints.
5. The clay can be preserved for modeling by wrapping in plastic and placing in a refrigerator.

NOTE: Various materials may be added for details.

Supplies

1. White glue
2. Bread
3. Lemon juice
4. Paint (watercolor, tempera, acrylic)
5. Brush
6. Plastic bag

Carved Plaster Bas-relief

Supplies

1. Cardboard container to be used as a mold (paper plate, lid or bottom of a box, etc.)
2. Molding plaster
3. Container for mixing plaster
4. Carving tool (scissors, knife, chisel, nail, etc.)
5. Pencil and paper
6. See procedure seven for supplies used in finishes

Procedure

1. Mix the plaster as follows:

   a. Pour the desired amount of water in the mixing container.
   b. Add the plaster to the water by sifting it through the fingers or gently shaking it from a can or small cup.
   c. Continue adding the sifted plaster to the water until the plaster builds up above the surface. Allow to soak twenty to thirty seconds to thoroughly blend the mixture.
   d. Stir the plaster thoroughly with the hands until it is smooth and creamy, making sure that any lumps of plaster are broken. Stir gently to avoid bubbles.
   e. Once the plaster is mixed do not add more water to thin, or more plaster to thicken, because the same consistency cannot be regained.
   f. Pour the plaster into the cardboard container which is to be used for the mold. Agitate the mold gently to bring any bubbles to the surface.

   NOTE: Begin to clean up immediately after pouring the plaster in the mold—it will harden rapidly once the chemical reaction takes place. Any excess plaster remaining should be wiped from the pan immediately and rolled in newspaper so that it might be disposed of more easily. Do not wash plaster down any drain. When cleaning the hands, tools, and mixing pan, be sure the water runs continuously.

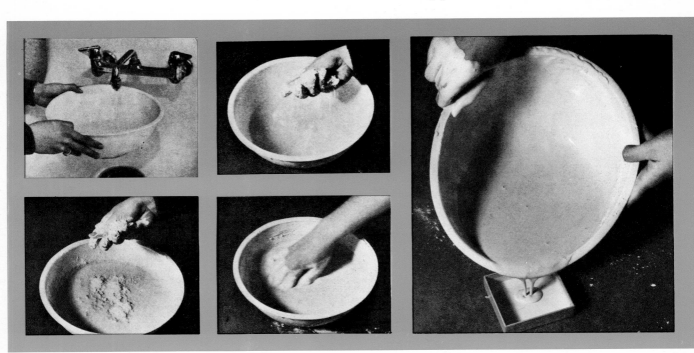

2. Allow the plaster to harden and dry thoroughly before removing the cardboard mold. Should some of the cardboard adhere to the plaster, wash it off under running water. A thin coating of vaseline will prevent the plaster from sticking to the box.
3. Smooth the sharp edges by scraping with any available tool.
4. Prepare a drawing to be transferred to the plaster.
5. Transfer the drawing to the plaster.
6. Carve the design into the plaster, using any suitable carving tool. Soaking the plaster in water will facilitate its carving. As plaster is very brittle, it is suggested that it be placed on a soft pad to avoid breakage.
7. Any of the following finishes can be applied to the carved plaster.

   a. If tempera paint decorations are applied to the plaster, clear plastic spray, shellac, or varnish can be painted over the surface for permanency.
   b. A pure white glossy finish can be achieved by soaking the plaster relief for approximately thirty minutes in a solution of dissolved white soap flakes and then wiping dry with a cloth.
   c. An antique finish can be obtained by soaking the plaster cast in linseed oil. The cast should then be removed from the bath, and while still wet, dusted with dry yellow ochre or umber. Wipe off any excess coloring with a cloth until the antique finish is suitable.
   d. The plaster plaque, when decorated with enamel or oil base paint, needs no protective finish.

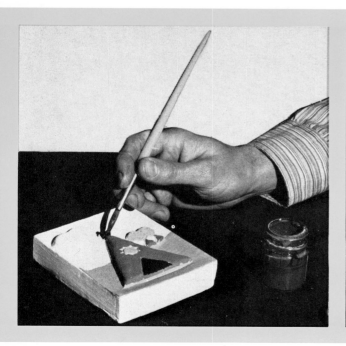 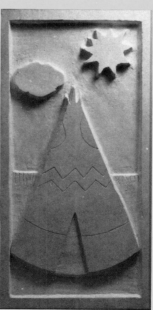 

Cast Plaster Bas-relief

Supplies

1. Cardboard container (lid or bottom of a box, paper plate, etc.)
2. Modeling clay (either water or oil base clay)
3. Modeling tool (orange stick, nail file, knife, etc.)
4. Molding plaster
5. Container for mixing plaster
6. Separating agent (salad oil, green soap, vaseline, etc.)
7. Brush
8. See procedure number nine for supplies used in finishing

Procedure

1. The container is to be used as a mold. Place it on a sheet of paper and trace around it with a pencil. This will provide a pictorial area of the same dimensions as the completed work. The preliminary drawing may be done in this area.
2. Fill half of the container with plastic clay.
3. Place the drawing over the clay in the container and transfer the drawing to the clay by tracing over the lines with a sharp pencil, pressing only heavily enough to make an impression in the clay.
4. Model or carve the design in the clay, making sure that none of the edges have undercuts.
5. Brush a thin film of oil on the clay to serve as a separating agent.
6. Mix the plaster as follows (see illustrations on pages 198 and 199):

   a. Pour the desired amount of water in the mixing container.
   b. Add the plaster to the water by sifting it through the fingers or gently shaking it from a can or small cup.
   c. Continue adding the sifted plaster to the water until the plaster builds up above the surface.
   d. Stir the plaster thoroughly with the hands until it is smooth and creamy, making sure that any lumps of plaster are broken. Stir gently to avoid bubbles.
   e. Once the plaster is mixed do not add more water to thin, or more plaster to thicken, because the same consistency cannot be regained.

7. Pour the plaster into the mold over the clay relief to the desired thickness. Agitate the container gently to bring any bubbles to the surface. A wire hook can be placed in the plaster before it hardens completely.

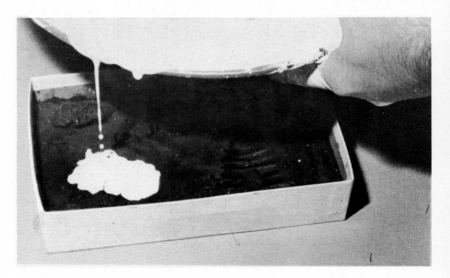

NOTE: Begin to clean up immediately after pouring the plaster in the mold—it will harden rapidly once the chemical reaction takes place. Any excess plaster remaining should be wiped from the pan immediately and rolled in newspaper so that it might be disposed of more easily. Do not wash plaster down any drain. When cleaning the hands, tools, and mixing pan, be sure the water runs continuously.

8. Allow the plaster to harden before removing the cardboard mold. Then remove the clay from the plaster. Apply the final finish after repairing any flaws that may appear in the plaster. Wash off any water base clay that adheres to the plaster.

9. Any of the following type finishes can be applied to the plaster.

   a. If tempera paint decorations are applied to the plaster, clear plastic spray, shellac, or varnish can be painted over the surface for permanency.
   b. A pure white glossy finish can be achieved by soaking the plaster relief for approximately thirty minutes in a solution of dissolved white soap flakes and then wiping dry with a cloth.
   c. An antique finish can be obtained by soaking the plaster cast in linseed oil. The cast should then be removed from the bath, and while still wet, dusted with dry yellow ochre or umber. Wipe off any excess coloring with a cloth until the antique finish is suitable.
   d. The plaster plaque, when decorated with enamel or oil base paint, needs no protective finish.

Container Sculpture

Supplies

1. Empty milk cartons or plastic containers
2. Knife, single-edge razor blade or scissors
3. Masking tape or glue
4. Tempera paint
5. Brush
6. Small amount of liquid detergent

Procedure

1. Make a decision as to the kind of sculpture desired (people, animals, machinery, buildings, cars, trucks, etc.).
2. Make the necessary cuts or cutouts with a cutting tool.
3. Fasten the parts together with tape or glue.
4. Paint if necessary. A few drops of liquid detergent added to tempera paint will allow paint to adhere to waxy surfaces.

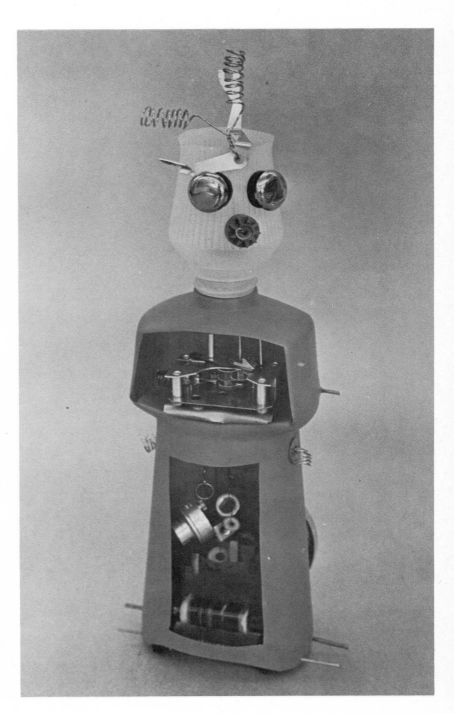

Foil Sculpture

Procedure

1. Crumple the foil into individual forms which, when assembled, will create a piece of sculpture.
2. Join these forms together with tape or straight pins.
3. Color can be added to the surface by painting with a drop or two of liquid detergent mixed in the tempera paint.

NOTE: See page 210, paper sculpture combined with foil sculpture, for additional ideas.

Supplies

1. Foil
2. Gummed tape or transparent tape
3. Brush
4. Liquid detergent
5. Tempera paint

Mobiles

Mobiles have been in existence for centuries in many countries. The Chinese glass windbells are probably the best known. A mobile is created to produce movement with changing patterns. In addition, a mobile is a problem in balance, design, sculpture, form, space, and color. Mobiles, like many other projects in this book, when simplified, are most successful in the primary grades.

Supplies

1. Thread
2. Supports (heavy stove pipe wire, small welding rods, strips of wood, or dowels)
3. Wire cutters
4. Glue
5. Materials for making objects to be suspended (paper, wire, plastics, cardboard, soda straws, plaster, clay, etc.)

Procedure

1. Decide the number of units to be used in the mobile and their method of construction. These objects can be made from paper, wire, papier-mâché, salt and flour, wood, etc., or a combination of any of these materials. Remember that an effective mobile should contain objects which have some kind of relationship to each other.
2. Attach a thread to each object so that it hangs evenly. This would make a finished mobile for the child in the primary grades.
3. Cut a support (a piece of wire or small wood dowel) and suspend an object from each end, making sure that the separation is great enough to prevent the parts from touching.
4. Place a spot of glue on the very ends of the wire or dowel to help hold the thread of each object when tied in place. The thread supporting the object should be comparatively short, but of different lengths.
5. Tie another thread to the wire or dowel supporting the mobile by the thread. Slide the thread back and forth on the wire or dowel until it finds a point of balance. Secure it with a spot of glue. This would be a complete mobile for older children. A mobile is built from the bottom up, so that this part will be the bottom if more pieces are to be added and the mobile is to become more complex.
6. The thread holding the section just completed should be tied to the end of another wire or dowel and held in place with glue. Suspend an object from the other end of the wire or dowel.
7. Balance both sections on a single thread.
8. Any number of sections can be added as long as balance is maintained.

NOTE: A wire stretched in a seldom used corner of the room will enable the children to hang their mobiles while working on them. There is no limit to the ways a mobile can be constructed, once the principle of movement and balance is understood.

Natural Object Sculpture

Supplies

1. Natural material (seeds, twigs, pine cones, seed pods, stones, driftwood, etc.)
2. Quick-drying glue
3. Clear quick-drying spray
4. Paint
5. Construction paper
6. Felt

Procedure

1. Collect a number of natural objects of various sizes and colors.
2. Arrange several of these items to create a small piece of sculpture.
3. When satisfied with the creation, glue it together.
4. Paint or colored paper can be added to enhance the sculpture.
5. Spray with clear spray to preserve the finish.
6. Glue a piece of felt to the bottom to prevent scratching.

Paper Sculpture

Paper generally is thought of in terms of two dimensions, such as flat cut out paper shapes fastened to a contrasting color sheet of paper. However, paper can be modeled into numerous three-dimensional forms after some experimentation. Any one or any combination of the following methods can be employed to produce fascinating paper sculpture.

Bending
Curling
Cutting
Folding
Fringing
Illusion of a solid
Joining
Perforating

Pinking
Pleating
Rolling
Scoring
Slitting
Twisting
Weaving

The following are examples of basic techniques which can be given many variations to suit the needs of the artist. Also see paper textures, pages 165 and 166.

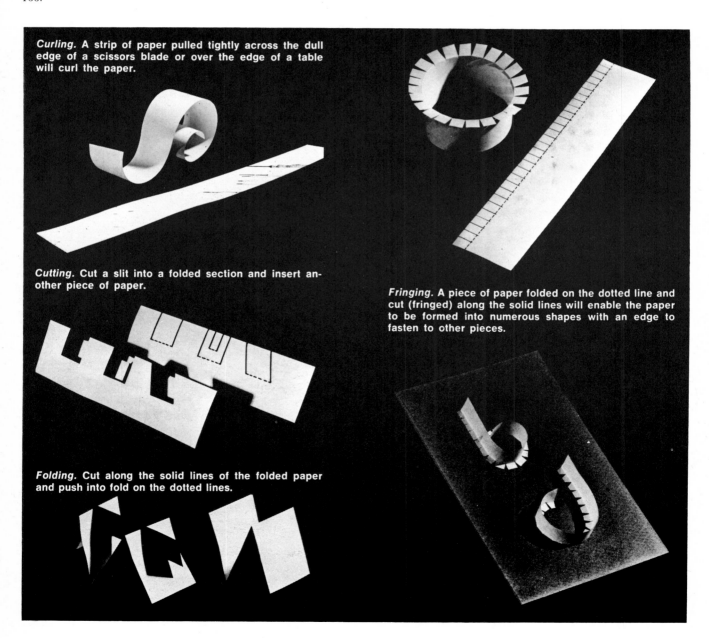

Curling. A strip of paper pulled tightly across the dull edge of a scissors blade or over the edge of a table will curl the paper.

Cutting. Cut a slit into a folded section and insert another piece of paper.

Folding. Cut along the solid lines of the folded paper and push into fold on the dotted lines.

Fringing. A piece of paper folded on the dotted line and cut (fringed) along the solid lines will enable the paper to be formed into numerous shapes with an edge to fasten to other pieces.

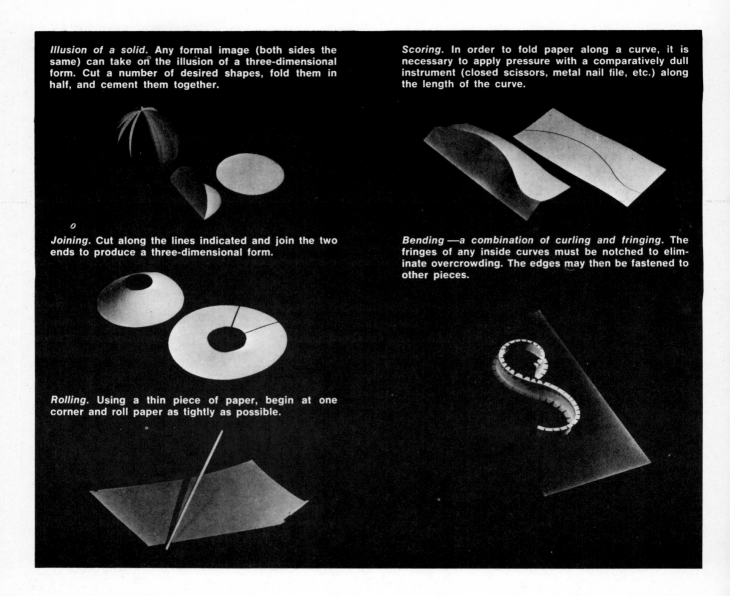

Illusion of a solid. Any formal image (both sides the same) can take on the illusion of a three-dimensional form. Cut a number of desired shapes, fold them in half, and cement them together.

Joining. Cut along the lines indicated and join the two ends to produce a three-dimensional form.

Rolling. Using a thin piece of paper, begin at one corner and roll paper as tightly as possible.

Scoring. In order to fold paper along a curve, it is necessary to apply pressure with a comparatively dull instrument (closed scissors, metal nail file, etc.) along the length of the curve.

Bending —a combination of curling and fringing. The fringes of any inside curves must be notched to eliminate overcrowding. The edges may then be fastened to other pieces.

Supplies

1. Paper. (There are many kinds of paper suitable for paper sculpture—rough, smooth, thick, thin, heavy, fragile, transparent, translucent, opaque, etc.; each has its own particular quality.)
2. Scissors, sharply pointed knife, or single-edge razor blade
3. Adhesive material (transparent tape, masking tape, rubber cement, library paste, etc.)
4. Fasteners (small staples, pins, paper clips, etc.)
5. A ruler, compass, or paper punch will be helpful

Procedure

1. Experiment with the numerous possibilties of shaping the paper into three-dimensional forms. Several such forms fastened together may result in fascinating figures, animals or birds. A textured surface can be accomplished by punching a series of holes in the paper or by cutting a series of small slits in the paper and then bending them either inward or outward to enrich the surface.

NOTE: There are a number of books in publication which deal exclusively with the three-dimensional possibilities of paper.

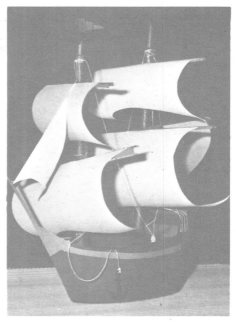

Paper Sculpture with Foil Sculpture

The combination of paper sculpture and foil sculpture lends itself to the creation of fascinating three-dimensional work. This is best discovered through experimentation with the two materials. See pages 207 to 209 (paper sculpture) and page 203 (foil sculpture) for suggestions.

Paper Tape Sculpture

Gummed paper tape is thought of in terms of its two-dimensional applications, such as taping shut a box for mailing. However, gummed paper tape can be modeled into numerous three-dimensional forms after some experimentation. Any one of the following methods can be employed to produce a fascinating piece of tape sculpture.

Bending	Joining (several pieces together)
Curling	Perforating
Cutting	Pinking
Fluting	Scoring
Folding	Twisting
Fringing	

Procedure

Experiment with the numerous possibilities of shaping the tape into three-dimensional forms. Several such forms fastened together may result in fascinating figures, animals or birds. A textured surface can be accomplished by punching a series of holes in the tape or by cutting a series of small slits in the tape and then bending them either inward or outward to enrich the surface.

Supplies

1. Roll of gummed paper tape (the tape, when moistened, will adhere to itself)
2. Scissors
3. Masking or transparent tape
4. Small sponge
5. Dish for water

Salt and Flour Sculpture

Supplies

1. One cup salt
2. One cup flour
3. One tablespoon powdered alum
4. Mixing bowl
5. Food coloring or dry tempera if color is desired
6. Shellac and brush
7. Alcohol for cleaning brush

Procedure

1. Mix 1 cup of salt, 1 cup of flour, and 1 tablespoon of alum to the consistency of putty, and add color if desired. Pinch pots, animals, and figures can be modeled from this mixture.
2. After the pieces have dried and hardened, they may be shellacked for permanence.

NOTE: See other formulae on pages 248 and 249.

Sawdust Sculpture

Supplies

1. Sawdust
2. Wheat paste
3. Brush
4. Tempera paint
5. Plastic spray or shellac

Procedure

1. Mix the sawdust and paste, and stir the mixture to the consistency of plastic clay.
2. Form the desired shape with the hands. An inner support of wire or wood is needed to brace large forms.
3. When dry, the sculpture can be painted with tempera paint.
4. A clear plastic spray or several coats of shellac will preserve the finish.

Soda and Cornstarch Sculpture

Procedure

1. Combine the ingredients (1 cup cornstarch, 2 cups baking soda, 1¼ cups water) in a saucepan and cook over medium heat, stirring constantly.
2. When the mixture is thickened to doughlike consistency, turn out on a piece of aluminum foil or on a breadboard.
3. Food coloring may be worked into the clay when it has cooled slightly.
4. Keep the clay in a refrigerator covered with aluminum or in a plastic bag to keep it pliable when not in use.
5. Clay may be rolled and cut into shapes or may be modeled into small shapes.
6. Watercolor or tempera may be used to paint the clay objects when they are thoroughly dry.
7. The painted objects may be sprayed with a clear plastic or clear shellac.

NOTE: If it is desired to hang these decorative shapes, a hole may be punched in the top of the ornament while the clay is soft or a Christmas ornament hook may be inserted in the back of the piece while the clay is soft.

Supplies

1. 1 cup cornstarch
2. 2 cups baking soda (1 lb. box)
3. 1¼ cups water
4. Saucepan
5. Stove or hot plate
6. Aluminum foil
7. Food coloring
8. Plastic bag
9. Watercolor or tempera paint
10. Clear commercial spray

Soda Straw Relief

Supplies

1. Drinking straws
2. Cardboard
3. Glue
4. Scissors
5. Box (to catch cut straws)

Procedure

1. Make an outline drawing on cardboard with pencil.
2. Cut the straws into a box and glue them perpendicularly to the cardboard, filling in areas or following pencil lines.

NOTE: Straws of one length simplify the procedure, but straws of various lengths will create more interest. Straws may be combined with flat areas of construction paper to produce the image or add interest.

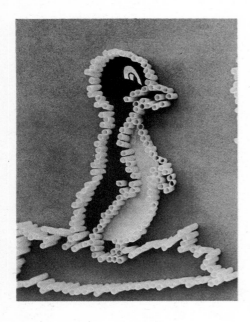

Spool Sculpture

Procedure

There can be no prescribed procedure in this project, as each of the figures is made differently, according to the imagination of the artist. Basically, the procedure involves "dressing" the spool, which serves as a body. The materials are contrived to serve as clothing, and are adhered to, or sewn around, the spool. Many extras can be added, as shown by the illustrations. Facial features are usually added with drawing materials (pen, pencil, crayon, etc.). Doll hair may be used to crown the figure, or the hair may be fabricated from thread, string, or anything suitable.

Supplies

1. Spools (a variety of sizes are useful)
2. Assorted fabrics
3. Needle and thread
4. Glue
5. Anything which will serve to simulate clothing accessories and other adornments

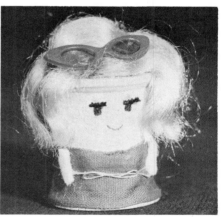

Stuffed Newspaper Sculpture

Supplies

1. Newspaper or newsprint
2. Glue or rubber cement
3. Paint (tempera, latex, watercolor, etc.)
4. Brush
5. Container for water
6. Clear spray, if necessary

Procedure

1. Cut shape of intended design from at least four pages of newspaper.
2. Glue two of the shapes together.
3. Glue the remaining two pieces together.
4. Glue the edges of these two sets together, leaving a space of approximately four inches unglued somewhere along the edge. Allow the glue to dry thoroughly.
5. Stuff crumpled paper through the four-inch opening until the design takes a three-dimensional form. Be careful not to tear the design by stuffing too tightly.
6. Glue the opening together.
7. Paint the surface, and spray with clear spray to keep paint from smudging.

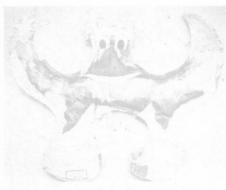

Toothpick Sculpture

Procedure

1. Glue the toothpicks together to form various three-dimensional structures.

   NOTE: Colored paper areas may be added as an experience in color and design.

Supplies

1. Quick-drying glue, such as house-hold cement
2. Toothpicks

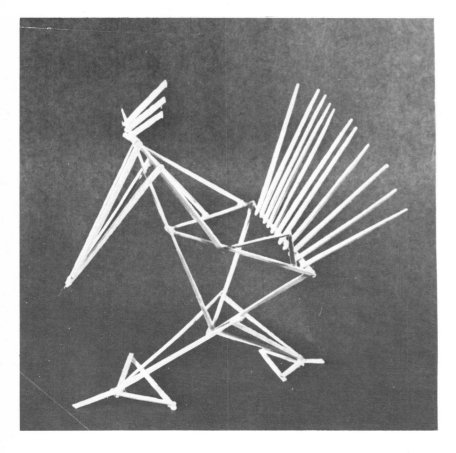

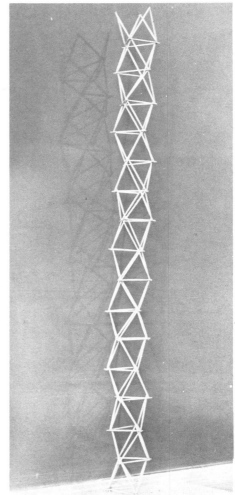

Wire Sculpture

Supplies

1. Any substantial wire with some flexibility, including heavy stovepipe, copper, aluminum, or bailing wire
2. Tool for cutting wire

Procedure

1. Decide on a design or figure which can serve as a subject. It may prove helpful to use a pencil sketch, but it should be remembered that the drawing must be purely linear. Remember also that the drawing is to be transformed into a three-dimensional work and should not be followed too literally.
2. Bend and twist the wire into the desired shapes. Coils may serve as figure elements and these may be created by wrapping the wire around such objects as sticks, pencils, bottles, etc. Make sure the objects can be removed.
3. Wire sculptures are generally conceived as one continuous length of wire, but they may consist of several lengths joined together. If several pieces are used, they may be hooked, wound, or soldered together.
4. Paint may be added if it is felt that color will improve the appearance of the work. Other materials, that is, wood, sponge, plastics, etc., may also be combined with the wire.

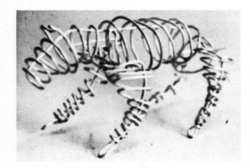

Wood Scrap Sculpture

Procedure

1. From a generous supply of small pieces of scrap wood of various sizes and colors, choose those pieces which will work well together in creating a piece of sculpture.
2. When the arrangement is satisfactory, glue all the components together.
3. Paint or crayon decorations can be added to finish the sculpture.

NOTE: A piece of sculpture should present interesting views from all sides.

Supplies

1. Scrap pieces of wood
2. Glue
3. Paints or crayons
4. Brush

STENCILS

Cutting a Stencil

Supplies

1. Stencil paper or a suitable substitute. The back of a typewriter stencil serves as a most satisfactory and inexpensive stencil paper. You can purchase a commercial stencil paper or make your own by drawing typing paper through paraffin melted in a flat pan (see page 250).
2. Cutting tool (single-edge razor blade, scissors, stencil knife, or mat knife)
3. Cutting board—heavy cardboard, old drawing board, old plate or mirror, or a small piece of heavy glass to protect the desk top when cutting stencils with a razor blade or knife. (A piece of plate glass could serve as a cutting surface, a paint palette, and a block printing-inking surface. Safety would require that the edges of the glass be covered heavily with tape.)

Procedure

1. Lay the stencil paper over a drawing. Trace the parts you wish to cut out if the design cannot be seen through the stencil. (Holding the stencil against a window is the easiest method.) As a general rule thin lines are not very visible in the final product.
2. Place the stencil paper on a sheet of heavy glass or cutting board and cut around the outlines. The paper from which the shapes have been cut is the negative stencil. The shapes which fall away from this stencil are the positive stencils.

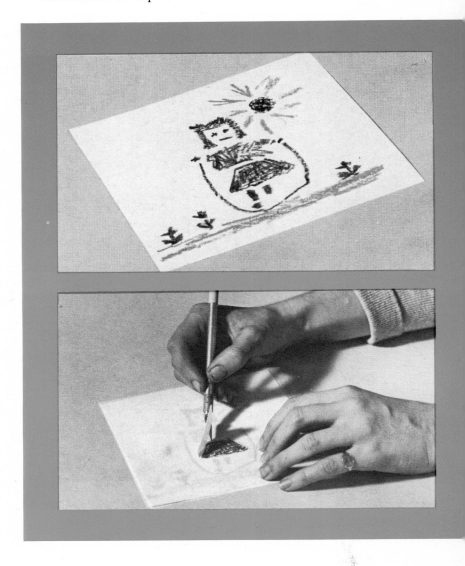

Crayon Stencil

Supplies

1. Stencils
2. Wax crayons
3. Paper
4. Eraser
5. Newspaper

Procedure

1. Cut the stencil as directed on pages 222 and 223.
2. Lay the stencil on a sheet of newspaper and crayon heavily on the stencil paper and around the edge of the design. The back of a typewriter stencil serves as a most satisfactory and inexpensive stencil paper. You can purchase a commercial stencil paper or make your own by running typing paper through paraffin melted in a flat pan.
3. Hold or fasten the stencil firmly in place over the drawing paper.
4. Transfer the crayon from the stencil onto the other paper with an eraser.

NOTE: Crayon may be stroked directly through the stencil onto the other paper as described under chalked stencils (page 228).

Spattered Stencil Design

Procedure

1. Cut the stencil as directed on pages 222 and 223.
2. Use the tape to fasten the paper in the center of the sheet of newspaper.
3. Pick up a small quantity of paint or ink with the brush (excess paint or ink will destroy the fine spatter effect).
4. Hold the screen above the paper and rub back and forth across it with the brush. In the absence of window screen, one may get similar results by drawing a stick across the brush bristles away from the paper.

NOTE: A little experimentation on scrap paper is recommended before attempting the finished product.

It is possible to reproduce the image of various forms of plant life by simply pinning them to the drawing paper and spraying over them.

Supplies

1. Tempera paints or colored inks
2. Stencil paper
3. Drawing paper
4. Small piece of window screen
5. Stiff bristle brush, such as an old tooth brush
6. Tape
7. Newspaper or wrapping paper

Sponged Stencil Design

Supplies

1. Stencil paper
2. Tempera paint or colored ink
3. Small piece of sponge
4. Drawing paper
5. Clip-type clothespin

Procedure

1. Cut the stencil as directed on pages 222 and 223.
2. Pick up the sponge with the clothespin or fingers, and dip it in the paint, making sure that the sponge is not fully saturated.
3. Put the stencil over the paper, hold or fasten it securely, and press the sponge lightly enough to utilize the sponge texture over the open portions of the stencil. Avoid scrubbing with the sponge, as this will work the paint under the stencil, creating ragged edges.

NOTE: A little experimentation on scrap paper is recommended before attempting the finished product.

Sprayed Stencil Design

Procedure

1. Cut the stencil as directed on pages 222 and 223.
2. The paper to be sprayed should be fastened to a newspaper or piece of wrapping paper. Secure the stencil over this so that it lies perfectly flat.
3. Place the newspaper on the floor, or tape it to the wall so that the stencil is at a convenient height.
4. Spray over the stencil, making sure that the open areas are fully covered with the paint.

NOTE: Variety may be added by spraying some areas more heavily than others, by using different colors on the shapes, or overlapping the colors. In overlapping colors, it is generally advisable to permit complete drying of the first coat before attempting another.

It is possible to reproduce the image of various forms of plant life by simply pinning them to the drawing paper and spraying over them.

Supplies

1. Thinned paint or ink, or quick-drying commercial paint spray can
2. Stencil paper
3. Insect sprayer, fixative sprayer, or atomizer
4. Drawing paper
5. Newspaper or wrapping paper
6. Tape or pins

Positive Stencil   Sprayed Design

Stencil with Chalk

Supplies

1. Stencil paper
2. Chalks
3. A piece of cotton or cleansing tissue (finger may be used)
4. Paper

Procedure

1. Cut the stencil as directed on pages 222 and 223.
2. Lay the stencil over the paper. Hold or fasten it firmly in place.
3. If you are using the positive stencil, make a series of strokes with the chalk, working from the outside of the opening in, so as not to curl the edges of the stencil.
4. If the negative, or the cut-out stencil, is being used, stroke from the inside of this stencil out, to avoid the curling of stencil edges. This system will also prevent the chalk from sifting under the stencil.
5. If a softening effect is desired, rub the chalk lightly with the piece of cotton or tissue, or with the fingers, being careful to rub from the stencil onto the surface of the paper.

NOTE: The chalk may be applied directly to the paper with the cotton or tissue. Simply make strokes with the chalk on paper, and then pick up the chalk dust with the tissue or cotton, and proceed as directed in step four.

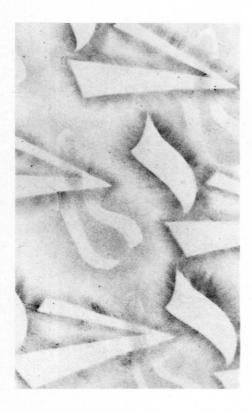

Stencil with Tempera

Procedure

1. Cut the stencil as directed on pages 222 and 223.
2. Hold or fasten the stencil securely in place.
3. Dip the stencil brush very lightly into the paint and wipe the excess paint from the brush onto a paper towel or absorbent cloth. The brush should appear to be almost dry, for very little paint is needed.
4. Apply the paint with strokes, which start on the stencil and run off onto the paper, or dab, with the brush held vertically to prevent any paint from getting under the stencil.

NOTE: Try overlapping these or new shapes with new colors for a more interesting design.

Supplies

1. Tempera paints
2. Stencil paper
3. Paper
4. Stencil brush (a brush with *short, stiff* bristles)
5. Jar of water and absorbent cloth for cleaning brushes
6. Tray for mixing paints

Textile Painting with Stencils

Supplies

1. Stencils
2. Drawing board or flat smooth surface to which fabric can be tacked for stenciling
3. Thumb tacks
4. Paper towels or absorbent cloths
5. Fabric which has been washed to remove sizing (linen, sail cloth, muslin, gingham, etc.)
6. Textile paints
7. Stencil brushes, preferably one for each color, with short, stiff bristles
8. Textile cleaner (usually included with commercial textile paint)

Procedure

1. Cut stencil as directed on pages 222 and 223.
2. Press the cloth with a hot iron to remove any wrinkles. Tack the cloth to the drawing board or any other flat smooth surface.
3. Place the stencil in position on the cloth and tack it so that the stencil will not slip or slide on the material.
4. Touch the brush lightly in the paint; it is *especially* important in textile painting that a very, very small amount of paint be used. Too much paint will soak through the fabric and wash out when the material is laundered.
5. Wipe all of the excess paint from the brush with a paper towel or absorbent cloth. Running the brush back and forth across the towel or cloth will remove the excess paint and will also work the paint into the brush. The brush will appear to be nearly dry.
6. If an open stencil is being used, stroke or stipple with the brush, working from the outside of the opening in, so as not to curl the edges of the stencil. If you are using a positive stencil, stroke from inside of the shape out; this will prevent the paint from going under the edges of the stencil.
7. Experimentation will help to determine the proper quantity of paint to be used. It will be found that the shading or painting of one color over another in parts of the stencil will greatly enrich the design.
8. After stenciling all parts of the design (many colors may be used, but a separate stencil must be cut for each color), remove the stencil.
9. If the proper amount of paint has been used, the painted fabric will appear to be dry and the paint will not have soaked through the material. For all practical purposes the fabric is now dry enough for handling; however, the paint should be allowed to dry thoroughly overnight before pressing with a hot iron for permanence. Be sure to read the directions on your textile paint to complete this last step.
10. Clean the brushes with a textile cleaner.

Weaving and Macramé have been gaining in popularity over the past few years, and would be of interest to the art supervisor; unfortunately, they are areas which are too comprehensive and complex to be effectively covered in this book. The reader is referred to the many good books in this area now on the market.

Applique

Supplies

1. A piece of loosely woven material cut to the size and shape of the finished picture (colored burlap is most satisfactory, as the open weave makes stitching easier)
2. Materials to be appliquéd to the background cloth (felt, or any other type of material which will not ravel or fray too easily)
3. Large blunt needles
4. Thread, colored yarn, raffia or string for stitching
5. Scissors

Procedure

1. The edges of the background material may be fringed before starting the picture. This will give a more finished look to the piece.
2. When the design has been decided upon, the shapes to be used in the picture may be cut and laid on the background until the arrangement is satisfactory.
3. The pieces of cloth are appliquéd to the background by using a variety of stitches chosen by the designer. A long running stitch or an overcast stitch are perhaps the easiest for small children to use.
4. The picture may be pressed with a warm iron when finished.

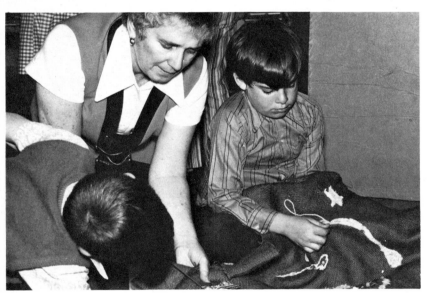

Cloth Batik

Supplies

1. Material to be decorated
2. Smooth board
3. Pencil and paper
4. Thumbtacks or staple gun
5. Carbon paper
6. Wooden frame or picture frame in the size of finished batik
7. Paraffin and beeswax
8. Old pan or can for melting wax
9. Toluene—keeps wax from congealing too quickly (should be available locally)
10. Electric hot plate, or 150 watt electric light bulb
11. Brush
12. Dye
13. Bowl for mixing dye
14. Iron
15. Newspaper or wrapping paper

Procedure

1. Develop a full-scale drawing with pencil on paper.
2. Stretch the material tightly on a smooth board. Fasten it with thumbtacks or a staple gun.
3. Transfer the design from the paper to the cloth with pencil and carbon paper.
4. Remove the cloth from the board, and stretch it tightly over the wooden frame. Fasten with thumbtacks or staple gun.
5. Melt equal parts of paraffin and beeswax together in an old pan over an electric hot plate, or 150 watt light bulb. Wax need not be boiling—use only enough heat to render the wax liquid.
6. Add a quantity of toluene equal to the paraffin and beeswax—this will keep the wax from congealing too quickly. (Toluene is extremely volatile and should be handled with caution.)
7. Place the frame on newspapers with the cloth side up.
8. Paint the melted wax on the cloth in areas that are to remain the natural color of the material. Make sure the wax penetrates through the cloth.
9. Remove the material from the frame. Crumple and submerge the material in the bowl of colored dye. Crumpling makes the crackle effective in the finished batik. Allow the cloth to dry.
10. Stretch the material on the frame again for each additional color that is needed.
11. Paint the melted wax over the areas just dyed to retain this color. Remove the cloth from the frame and dye it in a second color. This operation can be repeated several times.
12. Remove the wax from the material in boiling water or by ironing it between newspapers or wrapping paper. If using the iron for wax removal, change the papers often.

NOTE: Clean the brush with turpentine and soap, or detergent.

Cotton Roving

Procedure

1. Cover working area with newspaper.
2. Place construction paper on newspaper and cover large area of the construction paper with heavy layer of paste.
3. Lay the desired colored roving in the paste as if drawing an outline. Do not stretch the roving when applying.
4. Cut the roving when shape is completed.
5. Gently pat the roving into the paste.
6. Continue with a second line of roving inside the first outline.
7. Continue until desired result is obtained, changing colors if necessary.

NOTE: Roving can also be wrapped around a paste-covered shape cut from cardboard.

Supplies

1. Cotton roving (inexpensive, bulky cotton yarn)
2. Paste or media mixer (page 247)
3. Newspaper
4. Paste applicator (brush or piece of cardboard or folded paper)
5. Scissors
6. Cardboard or construction paper

Felt Picture

Supplies

1. Colored felt
2. Scissors
3. White glue or textile glue
4. Needle and thread (if design is to be sewn)

Procedure

1. When a design has been decided upon, the shape to be used in the picture may be cut directly from the felt or patterns can be made of cardboard.
2. Arrange the cut pieces of felt on a felt background until satisfactory.
3. Glue or sew the pieces in place to complete picture.

Melted Crayon Batik and Print

Procedure

1. Fasten cloth to board with masking tape, stretching the cloth as tightly as possible.
2. Draw a design on the cloth with a soft pencil.
3. Hold the crayon briefly over the flame of the candle until the crayon softens.
4. Press, drag, or drip softened crayon on the drawing.
5. A number of different colors can be used to complete the design.
6. Should crayon become too short to hold over the candle flame, a long pin stuck into the crayon will solve the problem.
7. The cloth can then be dyed with dye mixed in bowls as indicated on the box (see no. 13 for painting a design).
8. Remove cloth from the board, dip in water (crumple if crackle effect is desired), and place in dye solution, stirring constantly with stick or hand (use rubber gloves).
9. Remove from dye, rinse in cold water, and allow to drip dry or wring out excess water.
10. Place dyed cloth on pad of newspaper and cover design with a piece of paper. Cover with newspaper and iron until the crayon is transferred to the paper.
11. Remove the newspapers and printing paper, and a crayon print will be revealed (only one print can be made).
12. Store excess dye in an airtight glass container for further use.
13. Instead of dipping the cloth in the dye, various colored dyes can be painted over the crayon picture on the cloth. The crayon, being greasy, will resist the dye, to make interesting effects.
14. Rinse in cold water, and allow to drip dry or wring out excess water.
15. Press with hot iron when cloth is still damp.

NOTE: As this project involves the use of an open flame, it is suggested that every precaution be observed.

Supplies

1. Wax crayons, with paper wrapping removed
2. Paper
3. Candle
4. Cloth—muslin or any material that will easily absorb dye (old bed sheets are good)
5. Masking tape
6. Commercial dye, and sticks for stirring
7. Large glass jars (for storing dye)
8. Glass or enamel cooking utensils for mixing dye
9. Wooden board or heavy cardboard
10. Iron
11. Soft pencil
12. Brush
13. Rubber gloves
14. Newspaper

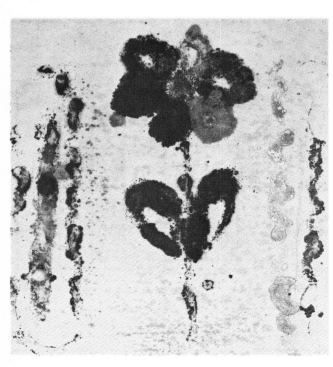

Paraffin Batik

Supplies

1. Paraffin
2. Electric skillet
3. Muffin tin
4. Brush
5. Cloth—muslin or any material that will absorb dye easily (old bed sheets are ideal)
6. Masking tape
7. Commercial dye, and sticks for stirring
8. Large glass jars (for storing dye)
9. Glass or enamel cooking bowls for mixing dye
10. Wooden board or heavy cardboard
11. Newspapers
12. Iron
13. Soft pencil
14. Rubber gloves
15. Baking soda (to extinguish any flames that may break out)

Procedure

1. Fasten cloth to board with masking tape, stretching the cloth as tightly as possible.
2. Draw a design on the cloth with a soft pencil.
3. Put water into skillet and muffin tin into water of skillet to form a double boiler.
4. Place pieces of paraffin in muffin tin and melt.
5. Brush in desired portions of the drawing with liquid wax (portions painted with wax will remain the cloth of the cloth).
6. The cloth can then be dyed with dye mixed in bowls as indicated on the box.
7. Remove the paraffin painted cloth from the board, dip in water (crumple if crackle effect is desired) and place in dye solution, stirring constantly with stick or hand (use rubber gloves).
8. Remove from dye, rinse in cold water and allow to drip dry. If second color is to be used, repeat no. 5 (but paint melted wax over desired areas just dyed), no. 7, and no. 8.
9. Place dyed cloth on pad of newspaper and cover with a pad of newspaper and iron to remove wax.
10. Change newspaper pads often until all wax has been removed.
11. Rinse in cold water, and allow to drip dry or wring out excess water.
12. Press with hot iron when cloth is still damp.
13. Store excess dye in an airtight glass container for further use.

NOTE: As this project involves the use of an electric skillet and liquid wax, it is suggested that every precaution be observed.

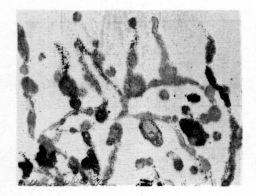

Stitchery

Procedure

1. Remove the selvage (the edge on either side of a woven fabric finished to prevent ravelling) and pull the threads on the burlap so the sides are straight.
2. Put a dab of white glue on each corner to prevent unravelling.
3. Pull interior threads and fill vacated space with colored yarn.
4. Patterns and variations can be achieved by going over two warp threads, under one, or any other combination.
5. Felt or fabrics can be appliquéd.
6. Various stitches, such as chain stitching, can be used.

NOTE: Additional fringing can be added at the bottom for wall hangings. Small curtain rods, doweling, or sticks can be attached to the top so the material will be held straight and can be attached to the wall.

Supplies

1. Colored burlap
2. Assorted colors and sizes of yarn
3. Tapestry needle

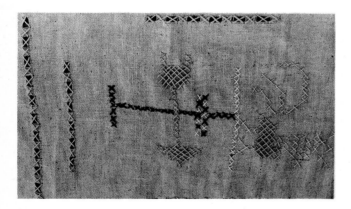

Tie and Dye

Tied and dyed material is made by dipping cloth in a dye bath after having wound parts of the cloth tightly with string or cord. The tightly wound string prevents the color dye from reaching parts of the fabric, creating a resist retaining the original color of the cloth. The tied and dyed method is suitable for numerous possibilities, including scarfs, blouses, T-shirts, aprons, etc.

Supplies

1. Enamel, glass, copper or brass cooking utensil
2. Jars for storing dye
3. Sticks for stirring dye
4. Hot plate
5. Iron to press finished material
6. Commercial dyes
7. Cloth—muslin, silk or any material that will absorb dye easily
8. String or cord
9. Marbles, small stones or pieces of wood
10. Rubber gloves

Procedure for Tying

1. *Concentric squares*
   Fold materials on the two diagonals of the cloth shape and wind string tightly at intervals from the middle.
2. *Concentric circles*
   Pick up the cloth from the middle and fold as evenly as possible away from the middle point, tying string tightly around the cloth at several intervals. When dipped in dye, the areas where the string was tied will create concentric circles and remain the color of the cloth.
3. *Varied shapes*
   Marbles or pebbles tied in the cloth will create interesting effects. Blocks of hard wood cut in various shapes and tied in the cloth (so not so much dye is absorbed) also crceate different designs.
4. *Stripes*
   Roll the cloth into a small tube and tie it with strong knots. Cloth folded accordion-style, tied tightly with string at intervals, will also create stripes.

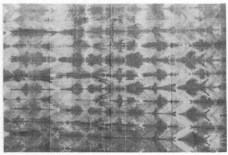

Procedure for Dyeing

1. The fabric to be dyed must be clean. Make sure all sizing is removed by washing vigorously with soap and hot water.
2. Plan your design by tying cloth in any combinations (Ill. 1). It may be wise to first experiment with a scrap piece of cloth.
3. Mix dye as indicated on box.

4. Dip material in warm water before dyeing. This will tighten the tied string and also conforms to the dyeing instructions on the dye box. Wring out excess water.
5. Place cloth in dye solution and stir constantly with stick or hand (use rubber gloves) so materials will be dyed evently (Ill. 2).
6. Leave the material in dye for only a few minutes or dye will penetrate the tied places.
7. Remove from dye and rinse in cold water (Ill. 3). Put dye in a glass container and keep for future use.
8. If another color is to be used, untie the strings desired, re-tie at other spots and put in next color dye solution.
9. Allow to drip dry or wring out excess water.
10. Press cloth with hot iron when cloth is still damp. This will also help set the color.

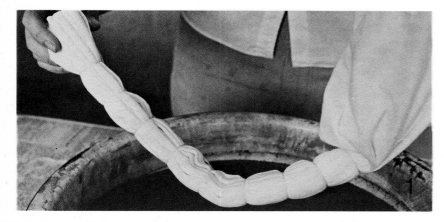

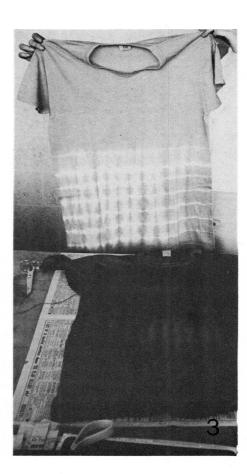

FORMULAS AND HINTS

Formulas and Hints

Antique Plaster Finish

Soak the plaster in linseed oil. Remove and dust with dry umber or yellow ochre while still wet. Wipe off excess with a cloth until antique finish is obtained.

Blown Eggs

Raw whole eggs can be emptied and the shells, when kept intact, can be decorated and used in many attractive ways.

With a needle, gently pierce a hole about the size of a grain of rice into both ends of a fresh raw egg. Make sure the yolk is broken.

Blow hard into one end of egg, which is held over a bowl, and the contents will leave the other end. (Save for scrambled eggs.)

Let water run inside the egg shell and rinse well until all of the contents of the egg is removed. Allow it to dry before decorating.

The holes at each end can be covered with melted paraffin or candle wax applied with an old brush.

Proceed to decorate with dye, ribbon, decorative braid, crepe paper, colored tissue paper, paint, beads, etc.

NOTE: Wax crayon drawn or melted wax painted on the surface of the egg will resist colored dye for interesting effects.
Dye the light colors first, then add more wax and dye darker colors.
A larger opening may be made in the front of the egg by first coating the area to be cut away with colorless nail polish. The opening then may be cut with sharp nail scissors. If the egg cracks around the opening, this can be covered with beads, braid, etc.
A scene or decoration may then be glued in place inside the egg. Such decorative eggs are especially nice on the Christmas tree or Easter tree.

Bread Dough Clay

Remove crusts from four slices of bread.

Tear bread into small pieces.

Mix pieces of bread with three tablespoons of white glue and two drops of lemon juice.

Allow one or two days for drying before decorating.

Preserve the clay in plastic bag and place in refrigerator.

Candle Wax

Wax from an old candle is best.
Paraffin alone is good but melts too rapidly.
Beeswax alone is excellent but too expensive.
Mutton tallow makes excellent hard candles, but becomes rancid.
Two formulas that work well are:
1. 60% by weight of paraffin
   35% stearic acid
   5% beeswax

2. 10 oz. mutton tallow
   4 oz. beeswax
   2 oz. alum
   ½ oz. gum camphor

Carving Gesso

Mix whiting and shellac to consistency of thick cream and add powdered tempera as needed to color.

Carving Material

1 part modeling plaster
1 part sawdust

Mix ingredients, then continue as illustrated on pages 198 and 199. Pour into a cardboard box and allow to harden. Soak block in water if it becomes too hard to carve.

Carving Paste

5 parts whiting
1 part liquid glue

Mix with water, thinning to the consistency of cream, and add powdered tempera for color.

Casting Cement

3 parts sand
1 part portland cement

Mix with water to a smooth consistency.

Drying Rack

Drying racks for wet art work are ideal if space is at a premium. A number of uniform wooden sticks tacked or stapled to uniform pieces of corrugated cardboard will make a drying rack. If pieces of wood are not available, substitute two, three, or four pieces of corrugated cardboard and tape together, then tape to the base cardboard.

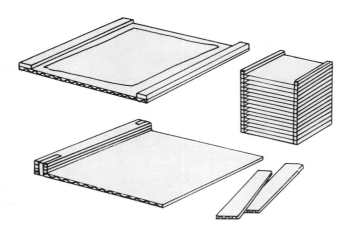

Encaustic Paint

1 oz. beeswax
2 teaspoons dry pigment or dry tempera for each color

Heat the beeswax and stir in the color with a stick.

Felt Applicator

A piece of felt held to a stick by a rubber band will ease application of chalk dust to a picture, and keep it a bit more permanent.

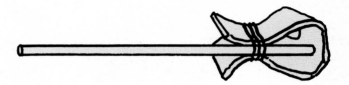

Finger Paint

1 cup liquid starch
6 cups water
½ cup soap chips (non-detergent)

Dissolve the soap chips in the water until no lumps remain, then mix well with the starch and remaining water. Color with dry or wet tempera or food coloring.

Mix wheat paste (wallpaper paste) into cold or lukewarm water. Stir until smooth. Pour into containers, one for each color, and stir in color pigment.

Small pieces of colored chalk finely ground and added to paste of a smooth consistency makes an inexpensive finger paint.
2 qts. boiling water and 12 tbsp. starch first dissolved in cold water. Stir until thick. Pour into containers, one for each color, and add pigments and a few drops of oil of clove to prevent distressing odors. Keep in cool place.

Fixative (to keep work from smearing)

Dissolve gum arabic in water to the consistency of thin cream. Spray through an insect sprayer or atomizer. Commercial hair spray may also be used.

Glossy Plaster Finish

Dissolve white soap flakes in a pan or bowl to the consistency of thin cream.

Soak the plaster cast or carving thoroughly in the solution for at least thirty minutes. Remove and polish with a dry cloth.

Hyplar Modeling Paste

(M. Grumbacher, Inc., New York). This is a water base paste, and dries and hardens quickly. It can be used for papier-mâché, modeled and shaped, carved, chiseled, or sawed when dry. The paste can be colored with acrylic watercolors that will dry to be waterproof.

Liquitex

(Permanent Pigments, Inc., Cincinnati, Ohio). A modeling paste with a water base, this is quick drying, and can be modeled, carved, tooled, textured and tinted with acrylic watercolor paint that dries to be waterproof. Thinned with water can be used for papier-mâché.

Methylan Paste

(The Standard Chemical Products, Inc., Hoboken, N.J.). This water base paste is colorless, odorless, non-staining, non-toxic and stays fresh indefinitely in a container that will not rust. It is suitable for use on papier-mâché, collage, découpage, etc. One-fourth pound makes approximately the same amount of paste as two pounds of wallpaper paste.

Modeling Cement

1 part portland cement
1 part asbestos cement
1 part powdered clay that has been sieved

Mix with water until of putty-like consistency.

Paint Container

Paper milk containers stapled together with tops removed and with a cardboard handle make an ideal container for colored paint and water.

Paint Dispensing

Plastic mustard or ketchup containers make good paint dispensers. An aluminum nail in the top of each will keep the paint fresh. In some cases the plastic containers can be used for painting. Syrup pitchers make good paint dispensers and are ideal for storing paint.

Parchment Paper

Brush the surface of a piece of cream-colored manila paper with burnt linseed oil; brush the back of the paper with turpentine and allow to dry.

Plastic Foam

6 tablespoons of plastic starch
1 cup dry detergent—for tinting, add powdered color

Mix with water and whip to consistency of marshmallow cream.

This can be used in decorating Christmas ornaments, puppet heads, etc.

Plastic Spoon

Keep plastic spoons in cans of powdered tempera for easy paint dispensing.

Prang Media Mixer

(American Crayon Company, Sandusky, Ohio). This water base mixer is a colorless, odorless, gelatin-like formula for converting liquid or dry tempera into colored finger paint. Used in a clear form, it will act as a binder for papier-mâché and as an adhesive for paper collage.

Printing Gimmicks

Glue heavy string or scraps of felt to a cardboard tube. Slip this tube over a painting roller so that it fits snugly. Roll it in paint and then over a piece of paper, possibly in various directions, to produce a design.

Salt and Cornstarch Clay

1 cup salt
½ cup cornstarch
¾ cup water

Cook in an old double boiler and in two minutes this will form a glob or mass. Place the mass on wax paper until it is cool enough to handle, then knead (as bread dough) for three minutes. The material can be wrapped in foil until time for use. It will keep several days, but must be kneaded again before using. It works well around wire or armatures.

Salt and Flour Clay

1 cup salt
1 cup flour
1 tablespoon powdered alum

Mix with water to consistency of putty.

Salt and Flour Gesso

2 cups flour
1 cup salt
1½ to 2 cups water

Mix until it is smooth and does not stick to the fingers.

Salt and Flour Relief Mixture

3 parts salt
1 part flour

Mix with water for desired consistency.

Salt Beads

2 parts table salt
1 part flour

Mix the salt and flour and water to a doughlike consistency. If color is desired add dry pigment or food coloring. Break off small pieces and form into beads. Pierce each with a toothpick and allow to dry, then string.

Sawdust and Wheat Paste for Modeling

2 parts sawdust
1 part wheat paste

Add paste to cold water to form a smooth and creamy mixture. Add sawdust and more water if necessary, until paste becomes like putty.

Silk Screen Paint

Combine liquid or powdered tempera mixed with a stiff mixture of soap flakes (not detergent) and warm water, or with Prang Media Mixer.

Simulated Marble

1 part Vermiculite
1 part modeling plaster

Mix ingredients and add water, stirring constantly until the mixture becomes creamy. Pour in cardboard box and allow to harden. Model with knife, rasp, sandpaper, or any similar tool.

Simulated Stone

Formula A

1 part sand
1 part cement
4 parts Zonalite
1 part modeling plaster

Mix ingredients, then add water to form a thick paste. Pour into cardboard, and allow to harden.

Formula B

2 parts sand
2 parts cement
4 parts Zonalite

Mix ingredients, then add water to form a thick paste. Pour into cardboard and allow to harden.

Soda and Cornstarch Clay

1 cup cornstarch
2 cups baking soda
1¼ cups water
Food coloring
Aluminum foil or plastic bag

Combine the first three ingredients in a saucepan and cook over medium heat, stirring constantly. When the mixture is thickened to doughlike consistency, turn out on a piece of aluminum foil or on a breadboard. Food coloring may be worked into the clay when it has cooled slightly.

Keep the clay in a refrigerator covered with aluminum fail or in a plastic bag to keep it pliable when not in use.

Clay may be rolled and cut into shapes or may be modeled into small shapes.

Stencil Paper

Typing paper pulled through melted paraffin in a flat pan makes an ideal stencil paper. Melt paraffin in a large, shallow pan over *very low* fire. Holding the end of the typing paper with tweezers, run the paper through the melted paraffin. Allow the paraffin to set by holding the paper over the pan for just a short time. Re-coat the paper in the same manner and allow to dry. Stencil paper is now ready to be used.

Sugar and Chalk

Dissolve about six tablespoons of sugar in a small container of water and soak chalk for about ten minutes before drawing or painting. When drawing or painting dries, it will be quite permanent.

Synthetic Oil Paint

Add dry color to regular wheat paste that has been mixed to thin, smooth consistency. Apply with a stiff brush.

Tempera Paint for Glossy Surfaces

Liquid detergent, or a few drops of glycerine mixed with tempera paint, enables the paint to adhere to shiny or oily surfaces, such as aluminum foil, glass, etc.

Translucent Paper

2 parts turpentine
1 part linseed oil

Brush or wipe the mixture on the paper and allow it to dry.

Transparent Paper

Two parts linseed oil and one part turpentine applied to the back of a drawing with a brush or rag will cause the illustration to become transparent.

Zonalite Sculpture Cement

1 part cement
5 parts Zonalite

Mix cement and Zonalite with water until smooth. Pour into a cardboard box or mold to harden. Zonalite cement is lightweight and can be cut with a saw or carved with any metal tool.

INDEX